T0323541

Voluntary Carbon Markets
Second Edition

Voluntary Carbon Markets
An International Business Guide to
What They Are and How They Work

Second Edition

Written and Edited by
Ricardo Bayon, Amanda Hawn
and
Katherine Hamilton

from Routledge

First published by Earthscan in the UK and USA in 2009

For a full list of publications please contact:

Earthscan
2 Park Square, Milton Park, Abingdon, Oxon OX14 4RN
711 Third Avenue, New York, NY 10017

Earthscan is an imprint of the Taylor & Francis Group, an informa business

ISBN: 978-1-844-07561-4 (hbk)
ISBN: 978-0-415-85198-5 (pbk)

Typeset by 4word Ltd, Bristol
Cover design by Andrew Corbett

A catalogue record for this book is available from the British Library

Library of Congress Cataloging-in-Publication Data

Voluntary carbon markets: an international business guide to what they are and how
they work / written and edited by Ricardo Bayon, Amanda Hawn and Katherine
Hamilton. – 2nd ed.
     p. cm.
  Includes bibliographical references and index.
  ISBN 978-1-84407-561-4 (hardback)
  1. Emissions trading. 2. Environmental impact charges. 3. Carbon dioxide
mitigation–Economic aspects. 4. Greenhouse gases–Economic aspects. 5. Climate
changes–Economic aspects.
  I. Bayon, Ricardo. II. Hawn, Amanda. III Hamilton, Katherine.
  HC79.P55V65 2009
  363.738'746–dc22
                          2008051841

Contents

List of Figures, Tables and Boxes

Figures

Tables

Boxes

List of Authors and Contributors

Authors

Ricardo Bayon is a partner and co-founder of EKO Asset Management Partners, a new breed of 'merchant bank' seeking to influence, encourage and profit from new and emerging markets for environmental commodities (carbon, water and biodiversity). The company invests in a variety of asset classes and types related to these new markets. Previously, Ricardo helped found and served as the Managing Director of the Ecosystem Marketplace. In that capacity he co-authored a number of publications on voluntary carbon markets. His most recent publication on markets for biodiversity is entitled *Conservation and Biodiversity Banking: A Guide to Setting Up and Running Biodiversity Credit Trading Systems*. For nearly two decades Ricardo has specialized in issues related to finance, banking and the environment. He has done work for a number of organizations including Innovest Strategic Value Advisors, Insight Investments, the International Finance Corporation (IFC) of the World Bank, the International Union for Conservation of Nature (IUCN), The Nature Conservancy and Domini Social Investment, among others. His articles have appeared in publications such as *The Washington Post*, *The Atlantic Monthly* and the *International Herald Tribune*. Ricardo was born in Bogota, Colombia, and is currently based in San Francisco.

Amanda Hawn is a Manager at New Forests, a Sydney-based financial services firm focusing on strategies for commercializing environmental assets and transacting in environmental markets. She leads client-based advisory work and contributes to New Forests' ecological product transactions. Prior to joining New Forests, Amanda was the managing editor of the Ecosystem Marketplace. She previously worked as a science journalist, covering the intersection of ecology and economics, with work appearing in *The New York Times*, *The Economist* and *Conservation Magazine*, among others. Amanda has a Bachelor of Science in ecology and evolutionary biology from Princeton University, a Masters in Zoology through a Princeton-in-Africa Fellowship at the University of Cape Town, and she is currently completing her MBA at the Haas School of Business at the University of California, Berkeley. Amanda is based in San Francisco with her husband, Nate, and a mutt named Maggie.

Katherine Hamilton is the Managing Director of the Ecosystem Marketplace. At the Ecosystem Marketplace, she has authored numerous pieces on carbon and water markets, as well as co-authoring the first, second and third annual *State of the Voluntary Carbon Markets* reports. Katherine has also co-authored book chapters and articles on environmental markets in a range of publications. Before joining the Ecosystem Marketplace, Katherine held positions at the Yale Environmental Law and Policy Center and the United Nations Development Program as a Hixon Center for Urban Ecology Fellow. She was also a founding staff member of Natural Capitalism Inc and worked for the International Council for Science as its programme coordinator for the United Nations World Summit for Sustainable Development preparations. Katherine holds a Masters in environmental management from Yale School of Forestry and Environmental Studies, where she wrote her thesis on the voluntary carbon markets, and a bachelor's degree from the University of Michigan. She is currently based in Washington DC.

Contributors

Lori Bird is a senior energy analyst with the National Renewable Energy Laboratory (NREL) in Golden, Colorado, specializing in the area of renewable energy markets and policy. She has co-authored a number of publications pertaining to green power and renewable energy certificate (REC) markets, utility green pricing programmes and renewable portfolio standards. Her work has appeared in academic and trade journals such as *Energy Policy*, *Renewable Energy World* and *Corporate Environmental Strategy*. She manages the Green Power Network, a web-based clearing house of information on green power products and consumer issues. Before joining NREL, she worked for the Department of Energy's Office of Energy Efficiency and Renewable Energy in Denver and for Hagler Bailly Consulting in Boulder, Colorado. She holds a Masters in environmental studies from Yale University's School of Forestry and Environmental Studies.

Dr David Brand is the founder and Managing Director of New Forests, a forestry asset management and advisory business based in Sydney, Australia (see www.newforests.com.au). The firm represents institutional and private equity investors in forestry and land management, specializing in investment programmes that can link to environmental markets related to carbon, water and biodiversity. New Forests also operates an advisory business that supports environmental market policies, business plans and transactions, advising both buyers and sellers of carbon offsets.

Martha Isabel Ruiz Corzo, a former music teacher, founded the Grupo Ecológico Sierra Gorda in 1989 along with her husband and a group of neighbours. The first director of the Grupo Ecológico, she led the effort to obtain the decree of the Sierra Gorda as a Biosphere Reserve, obtained in 1997. As a result of this, she was named by the President of Mexico as the first director of the Sierra Gorda Biosphere Reserve. A recognized social entrepreneur, Ruiz is an outspoken advocate for the development of payments for environmental services programmes that work in areas of extreme poverty. She is a member of the board of directors of Forest Trends.

Robert Harmon serves as Chief Innovation Officer and Senior Vice President for the Bonneville Environmental Foundation (BEF), where he is credited with developing BEF's Green Tag programme, which began in 1999. In 2000, BEF closed the first, large retail Green Tag transaction in the US. In 2001, Robert designed and launched BEF's CO_2 calculator, the first such calculator on the internet. In 2004, Robert was awarded the national Green Power Pioneer Award for his introduction of the retail Green Tag and his efforts to build a thriving and credible Green Tag market in the US. Robert has worked in the fields of energy productivity and renewables since 1987. He currently serves on the boards of the Northwest Energy Coalition and Green-e, the premier Green Power consumer protection programme in the US.

Ben Henneke is President of Clean Air Action Corporation (CAAC) and manages the International Small Group and Tree Planting Alliance (TIST) programme, in which subsistence farmers voluntarily plant trees to sequester carbon and create superior CO_2 offsets with biodiversity, desertification and economic development benefits. TIST is so popular with the farmers that it has been growing at over 100 per cent per year for the past five years. See www.tist.org.

Erin Meezan is the Assistant Vice President of Sustainability for Interface, Inc, the largest modular carpet manufacturer in the world and a leading sustainable business. She provides technical assistance and policy support to Interface's global businesses. She also manages Interface's partnerships with stakeholders and advises Interface's internal Sustainability Council. She oversees Interface's corporate greenhouse gas inventory and its carbon offset portfolio to meet corporate and product climate neutral goals. She has a Masters in environmental policy and a Juris Doctor from Vermont Law School.

Marisa Meizlish is the Manager of Advisory Services at New Forests. She has a BA in journalism and political science from Northwestern University in Chicago, and a Masters in environmental management from the University of New South Wales. Marisa previously worked in the news media and public relations fields in New York and Chicago.

Dr Janet Peace is the Director of Markets and Business Strategy at the Pew Center on Global Climate Change. In this role she manages the Center's Business Environmental Leadership Council (BELC), the largest US-based association of companies devoted to climate-related policy and corporate strategies, comprising 42 major corporations with combined market capitalization of $2.8 trillion. She also manages the Center's engagement with the Offset Quality

Initiative. Prior to taking on the director's role, Dr Peace was the Senior Economist with the Center, providing economic analysis of climate policy at the international, national and state levels. Before coming to Pew, Dr Peace was the Director of Offsets Development and Industry Relations with a Canadian non-profit group, Climate Change Central, and was a founding Chair of the National Offsets Quantification Team. In addition, she has taught environmental and natural resource economics at the University of Calgary, worked as a resource specialist with the US General Accounting Office, and served for a number of years as a geologist with the US Geological Survey. Dr Peace holds a Masters and PhD in economics and has an undergraduate degree in geology.

Dr Alexander Rau is a founding partner of Climate Wedge Ltd, an independent carbon finance and emissions trading advisory firm. Climate Wedge has partnered with Cheyne Capital to launch a multi-strategy carbon fund that manages a diversified global portfolio of high quality emissions reductions for use as carbon offsets by institutional buyers. Alex was previously part of the Climate Change Services team in PricewaterhouseCoopers's Energy Corporate Finance practice in London, helping develop and structure portfolios of carbon assets during the early stages of the Clean Development Mechanism (CDM) market. He has advised numerous clients such as McKinsey & Company, Rio Tinto, News Corporation, Électricité de France and the California Public Employees Retirement System (CalPERS) on carbon management and trading strategy. He also co-authored Version One of the Voluntary Carbon Standard, the most widely accepted trading standard for non-Kyoto carbon assets. Alex holds a PhD in physics from Oxford University and a BA from Cornell University.

David Ross, originally from the state of Ohio in the US, has worked for non-profit organizations for more than 18 years, including the American Civil Liberties Union of San Diego & Imperial Counties, the American Cancer Society, Butte Environmental Council, Parks & Preserves Foundation and National Wildlife Federation. He has been working on the project of biodiversity conservation in the Sierra Gorda Biosphere Reserve since 2003. He led negotiations on behalf of Bosque Sustentable for its sale of emission reduction credits to the United Nations Foundation.

Allison Shapiro is a Program Associate in the Carbon Markets programme of the Ecosystem Marketplace, where she focuses on the voluntary carbon markets. Prior to joining the Ecosystem Marketplace, she worked as a consultant at ICF International, where she contributed to various environmental consulting projects for federal government and commercial clients. Allison holds a BSc in science, technology and international affairs from Georgetown University.

Jonathan Shopley is CEO of The CarbonNeutral Company. Prior to joining The CarbonNeutral Company in 2001, he held the position of Managing Director and Vice President in the European division of Arthur D. Little, the technology and management consulting company. Before entering management,

Jonathan was an environmental engineer focused on the development of technologies for the mitigation of environmental impacts in industry.

Lorna Slade is with Group Corporate Affairs, HSBC Holdings plc. HSBC Holdings is developing a sustainability-focused business in a number of areas, particularly low carbon energy, water infrastructure, sustainable forestry and related agricultural commodities. It has also announced a strategy to help its clients respond to the challenges and opportunities of creating a lower carbon economy, advising them on the implications of climate change and the business opportunities that arise. In 2005, HSBC became the first bank to go carbon neutral.

Bill Sneyd is Director of Advisory Services at The CarbonNeutral Company, where he is responsible for advising clients on the development of their carbon management programmes and for representing The CarbonNeutral Company in developing standards for the voluntary carbon market. Bill has ten years of operational and consultancy experience in a variety of industries including energy and telecommunications, as well as climate change and carbon market experience. Prior to joining The CarbonNeutral Company, Bill spent two years with Diamond Cluster, a firm of management consultants specializing in the telecommunication and technology sectors. He began his career at Shell International as an operations engineer, serving the company in both The Netherlands and the US with a focus on plant maintenance, improving operational efficiency of production facilities, and offshore oil and gas fields in the Gulf of Mexico. Bill has a BSc in engineering and management from Durham University and an MBA from INSEAD, the international graduate business school. He is a Sainsbury Management Fellow and a Business Mentor for The Prince's Trust.

Dr Mark Trexler is the Director of Global Consulting Services for EcoSecurities, specializing in the provision of strategic, policy and market services to companies and governments around the world. He oversees a team of more than 20 EcoSecurities consultants, and works with EcoSecurities' 300 staff in 29 offices around the world. Dr Trexler has worked with global energy companies and consumer products companies, as well as national and international organizations. He began working on climate change in 1988 when he joined the World Resources Institute and has specialized in the field for 20 years. He has published extensively on issues related to climate change mitigation and has served as a lead author for the Intergovernmental Panel on Climate Change. Dr Trexler earned his Master of Public Policy in 1982 and his PhD in 1990 from the Graduate School of Public Policy at the University of California, Berkeley.

Ben Vitale is an experienced finance, operations and technology executive. He holds an MBA from Northwestern University's Kellogg School of Management and a BSc in computer and electrical engineering from Purdue University. Within Conservation International's Center for Environmental Leadership in Business, Ben is driving change to create new financial instruments for corporations, market makers and financing institutions to fully value and fund the ecological services provided by intact and restored ecosystems. In particular, he is working to develop investment grade Conservation Carbon projects in Madagascar, Ecuador, China, Brazil and other biodiversity hotspots.

Walker Wright is a consultant to the Terra Solar North America Group and Renewable Energy Solutions, Inc (RESI), two leaders in thin-film photovoltaic manufacturing and research. Walker focuses on business development and marketing and does not own a car. Walker holds a BA from Princeton University and an MSc from the London School of Economics.

Acknowledgements

Ricardo Bayon

Like most books, this one has been years in the making and has many parents. It was first born of the realization that, while there was much talk of the regulated carbon markets, the voluntary markets were being left behind. As soon as we began testing this hypothesis, we realized it was true. But knowing this should be done and getting it done were two very far-removed destinations. Getting the book to this stage would simply not have been possible without the unflagging support of Michael Jenkins and the rest of our colleagues at Forest Trends. Likewise, none of this would have happened were it not for the generous contributions of many donors to the Ecosystem Marketplace.

These include:

ABN-AMRO
Blue Moon Fund
Conservation International
The Citigroup Foundation
O Boticario
The David and Lucile Packard Foundation
The Gordon and Betty Moore Foundation
The Nature Conservancy
Surdna Foundation
The UK Department for International Development
The UK Forestry Commission
The US Forest Service; and
The US Natural Resources Conservation Service (NRCS)

Our deepest thanks to all of them for being more than sponsors; for being true partners.

Also, it should be mentioned that a tremendous amount of work that went into this book came from a report prepared for the Ecosystem Marketplace by David Brand and Marisa Meizlich at New Forests. Without that initial impetus, this book wouldn't have been possible. Likewise, I would like to thank, in no particular order, David Tepper, Richard Burrett, Mark Trexler, Mark Kenber, Renat

Heuberger, Richard Tipper, Jessica Orrego, Toby Janson-Smith, Jonathan Shopley, Bill Sneyd, Alex Rau, Michael Schlup and all of the contributors to this book for their openness and willingness to share both intelligence and information. Their excitement for these markets is contagious.

As anyone who knows them (and me) will tell you, this book would not be as good as it is if it weren't for my co-authors, Amanda Hawn and Katherine Hamilton. Their writing skills and insights make this book what it is. Last, but never least, I'd like to thank my wife Nathalie and son Luka for their support and forbearance. This book has meant many hours travelling and writing; hours away from them. Without a doubt, for me, this has been the most painful and costly part of the book's production process. May my time away from them in the future be brief.

Amanda Hawn

Many people helped with the creation of this book, but Peter Barnes and the managers of The Mesa Refuge – who provided the space to sit down and finally write – top the list of those to whom gratitude is due. All of the contributors to the fourth chapter of the book were generous with their time, energy and insight – for all of these things, the authors are thankful. In addition to those whose names appear as guest contributors, we are grateful to the many others who took the time to return phone calls, give interviews, provide statistics and generally enrich the information herein. We are grateful, too, to Marion Yuen who organized a great conference – the Green T Forum – about many of the topics covered in this book in May of 2006. Walker Wright and Nathan Larsen stayed up to burn the midnight oil during the final editing phases of the manuscript, and Rob West and his team at Earthscan were both patient and professional – thank you. Last but not least, I would like to extend my gratitude to my co-editors – Ricardo Bayon and Katherine Hamilton – who are as kind and professional, as they are intelligent.

Katherine Hamilton

In addition to the many supporters mentioned above, my gratitude goes to Brad Gentry and many others at the Yale School of Forestry and Environmental Studies, who first fostered my research on carbon markets. Many thanks also go to the numerous experts in this market, including Lars Kvale, Steve Zwick, Lori Bird, Ron Luhur, Hunter Lovins, Evan Ard, Marco Monroy, Eron Bloomgarden, Josh Margolis, Marcus Krembs, Onja Kollmus, Thomas Marcello, Reiner Musier, John Kunz and Lauren Kimble among others, who willingly took the time to educate, patiently answer questions, and offer insights into this evolving marketplace. I'm also appreciative for the continued support and inspiration from my co-authors Ricardo Bayon and Amanda Hawn. Finally, it is important to note the Second Edition of this book would have not been possible without the dedication and input of Allison Shapiro and Logan Rhyne at the Ecosystem Marketplace and our colleagues at Forest Trends – thank you.

Foreword

The serious debate over the climate crisis has now moved on from the question of whether it exists to how we can craft emergency solutions in order to avoid catastrophic damage.

The debate over solutions has been slow to start in earnest because some of our leaders still find it more convenient to deny the reality of the crisis. The hard truth for the rest of us is that the maximum that seems politically feasible still falls far short of the minimum that would be effective in solving the crisis.

T. S. Eliot once wrote:

> Between the idea and the reality, Between the motion and the act Falls the Shadow. Between the conception and the creation, Between the emotion and the response Falls the Shadow.

Leaders must try to shine some light on a pathway through this terra incognita that lies between where we are and where we need to go.

Outside of the Kyoto Treaty, business leaders in both political parties have taken significant steps to position their companies as leaders in addressing this crisis and have adopted policies that not only reduce CO_2 but make their companies zero carbon. Many of them have discovered a way to increase profits and productivity by eliminating their contributions to global warming pollution. A key contributor to the movement to freeze and then reduce carbon emissions and a remarkable area of commercial and policy innovation, is the voluntary carbon market.

Voluntary Carbon Markets by Ricardo Bayon, Amanda Hawn and Katherine Hamilton describes a remarkable area of innovation in the fight to control global warming pollution in describing the foundations upon which many promising carbon reducing strategies have been built. And in the current absence of a worldwide regulatory system for carbon reduction, *Voluntary Carbon Markets* also foreshadows the factors which will drive the next generation of market-based innovation for fighting global warming pollution. I commend the work of Ricardo and the Ecosystem Marketplace Group for jumping into T. S. Eliot's void and shining the light on this important market.

The climate crisis is not a political issue. It is a moral issue. It affects the survival of human civilization. It is not a question of left versus right; it is a question of right versus wrong. Put simply, it is wrong to destroy the habitability of our planet and ruin the prospects of every generation that follows ours.

What is motivating millions of global citizens to think differently about solutions to the climate crisis is the growing realization that this challenge is bringing us unprecedented opportunity.

This is an opportunity for transcendence, an opportunity to find our better selves and in rising to meet this challenge, create a better brighter future – a future worthy of the generations who come after us and who have a right to be able to depend on us.

Al Gore

List of Acronyms and Abbreviations

AB 32	California Global Warming Solutions Acts of 2006
ASA	Advertising Standards Authority (in UK)
BEF	Bonneville Environmental Foundation
CARB	California Air Resources Board
CBD	Convention on Biological Diversity
CCAR	California Climate Action Registry
CCBA	Climate, Community and Biodiversity Alliance
CCS	Carbon Capture and Storage
CCX	Chicago Climate Exchange
CDM	Clean Development Mechanism
CDP	Carbon Disclosure Project
CEI	Community Energy Inc
CER	Certified Emissions Reduction
CERES	Coalition for Environmentally Responsible Economies
CFCs	Chlorofluorocarbons
CFI	Carbon Financial Instrument
CO_2	carbon dioxide
COP	Conference of the Parties
CRS	Center for Resource Solutions
ECX	European Carbon Exchange
EPA	Environmental Protection Agency
ERT	Environmental Resources Trust
ERU	Emission Reduction Unit
EU ETS	European Union Emission Trading Scheme
EUA	European Union Allowance
FTC	Federal Trade Commission
GGAS	Greenhouse Gas Reduction Scheme
GHG	greenhouse gas
GPS	Global Positioning System
GSV	Gold Standard for Voluntary Emission Reductions
GWh	gigawatt hours
GWP	global warming potential
ICROA	International Carbon Reduction and Offset Alliance

IETA	International Emissions Trading Association
IPCC	Intergovernmental Panel on Climate Change
ISO	International Standards Organization
JI	Joint Implementation
kWh	kilowatt hour
LULUCF	Land Use, Land-Use Change and Forestry
MAC	California Market Advisory Commitee
MCeX	Montreal Climate Exchange
MDGs	Millennium Development Goals
Mt	million tons
MWh	megawatt hour
NECX	Northeastern Climate Exchange
NGAC	New South Wales Greenhouse Gas Abatement Certificate
NGO	non-governmental organization
NOx	Nitrogen oxides
NPA	Natural Protected Area (in Mexico)
NREL	National Renewable Energy Laboratory
NSW	New South Wales
NYCX	New York Climate Exchange
OTC	over-the-counter
PDA	personal digital assistant
ppm	parts per million
REC	renewable energy certificate
REDD	Reducing Emissions from Deforestation, Degradation
REN21	Renewable Energy Policy Network for the 21st Century
RFP	Request for Proposal process
RGGI	Regional Greenhouse Gas Initiative
ROCs	Renewable Obligation Certificates
RPS	Renewable Portfolio Standards
SO2	sulphur dioxide
SRI	Socially Responsible Investment
tCO_2e	metric tons of carbon dioxide equivalent
TIST	International Small Group and Tree Planting Alliance
UNEP	United Nations Environment Programme
UNFCCC	United Nations Framework Convention on Climate Change
VCS	Voluntary Carbon Standard
VCU	Voluntary Carbon Unit
VER	Verified Emissions Reduction
VERRs	Verified Emission Reduction Removal Credits
WBCSD	World Business Council for Sustainable Development
WCI	Western Climate Initiative
WRI	World Resources Institute
WWF	World Wildlife Fund

Introduction

After decades of searching for creative and innovative ways to protect the environment, it is time we be brutally honest with ourselves: we are losing this battle, and losing it in a spectacular way. Every day we hear that yet another species has gone extinct, yet another acre of forest has disappeared, and yet another coral reef has been destroyed. And as if that weren't enough, Earth has begun warming to such an extent that climate, sea levels, glacial ice and even the polar ice caps may be in danger. It is enough to demoralize even the most determined optimist.

But this is a battle we cannot afford to lose – literally. It is time not to give up, but to redouble our efforts, to become more creative, and to seek new ways of working together in situations where confrontation is no longer effective (if it ever was). The time, in other words, has come for the environmental equivalent of the St Crispin's Day speech in Shakespeare's *Henry V*, a call to arms that does not lament how difficult the task is likely to be – or how few of us there are – but rather pushes us forward into the wild and scary unknown.

And, in the case of the environmental movement, the scary unknown is the use of markets and market-like instruments to protect the environment. To be fair, we now have nearly two decades of experimentation in the use of market mechanisms for environmental protection. The US Acid Rain trading scheme began in the 1980s, and various forms of market-like mechanisms for environmental protection have been tried all over the world.

But the game is one of scale. Protecting one species, one piece of land, one watershed may be important, but it is no longer enough. The solutions today need to be systemic, they need to change the way we do business, the way we eat, drink, sleep and think. And this is where we think markets may hold the greatest promise.

Some years ago, we created Forest Trends with a vision. Our vision was simple: we believed that by bringing loggers, environmentalists, business people, academics and scientists together into the same room to think about issues that mattered to all of them we would be better able to stem the loss of the world's forests. But we soon realized that – effective as this might be – it was not enough. We saw that in order to save the world's forests, society needed to value standing forests as least as highly as it values soybeans, cattle ranches, logging operations and the other alternatives driving deforestation. As the saying goes, in the end, we will only protect what we value.

Initially, some of our friends in the environmental movement accused us of heresy. How could we want to put a value on nature? Nature, they felt, is and should always be priceless. And while we agree with the sentiment, in practice, our economic system doesn't see nature as priceless, it assigns it a value, a value that is awfully close to zero. In short, our society (or at least our economic system) is confusing priceless with worthless.

Having come to the realization that we needed to 'internalize the economic value' (to use the academic jargon) of nature, we quickly saw that one of the most effective ways to achieve this was through the use of markets or market-like instruments.

And so in 2000 we brought together a small group of people from around the world in the beautiful mountains of New South Wales, Australia, in a town called Katoomba, to discuss the role markets and payments for ecosystem services had to play in forest conservation. True to our roots, we made sure this group included people from all walks of life: bankers, business people, government officials, academics, community leaders, non-profits … the entire spectrum. And from this meeting was born the Katoomba Group. At that time few people were talking about markets and payments for ecosystem services. Remember, this was five years before the European Union's Emissions Trading Scheme was but a glint in anyone's eye. Even Kyoto, at the time, looked set to flounder.

In this way, the Katoomba Group became a stimulating place to refine our vision, define our strategies, and so we continued to meet once or twice a year in either a large market for forest goods and services (London, Tokyo, Switzerland), or a large producer of these services (Brazil, Vancouver, Thailand). As time went by the group grew and our understanding of our subject deepened. We realized that what we were talking about went much further than forests, that it was a systemic problem affecting all ecosystems, and we realized that in order to thrive, environmental markets need science, finance, expertise, and, most especially, information. That is why we created the Ecosystem Marketplace, a tool that we hope will become a central resource of news, data and analytics for the world's environmental markets.

All of this is a long-winded attempt to give you a bit of the background for the book you now hold in your hands. It was born of environmental need and it seeks to further deepen our understanding of one portion of the carbon markets that we think has been grossly overlooked: the voluntary carbon market.

But it is part of something bigger, part of our attempts to come up with (and better understand) a series of tools – environmental markets and market-like mechanisms – that may help us succeed where other tools have so far failed to conserve the ecosystems on which we all depend. So, once more into the breach, but this time, let's arm ourselves in the most effective way possible. Let's use markets – both voluntary and regulated – and payments for ecosystem services where they make sense to help us address climate change and other seemingly insurmountable problems. Because – as King Henry said at Agincourt – one day, we will look back and either be happy we did, or else wish we had; the choice is ours.

Michael Jenkins
President,
Forest Trends

Ricardo Bayon
Advisory Committee Chair,
Ecosystem Marketplace

1

The Big Picture

In 2005, Kerry Emanuel, a professor of atmospheric science at MIT, published a controversial paper in *Nature* linking global warming with the rising intensity of hurricanes (Emanuel, 2005). The paper relied on historical records showing that the intensity of Atlantic storms had nearly doubled in 30 years. What caught people's attention, however, was not this alarming statistic, but rather that it was released just three weeks before Hurricane Katrina displaced 1 million people and left an estimated 1836 dead.

For hurricane watchers, 2005 was indeed a year for the record books. A startling number of hurricanes hit the Gulf of Mexico, causing over US$100 billion in damages. The 2004 hurricane season was a bit less horrific in terms of raw numbers, but what it lacked in quantity, it made up for in oddity. The year was marked by an event some believed to be a scientific impossibility – a hurricane in the southern Atlantic Ocean. For over 40 years, weather satellites circling the globe had seen hurricanes and cyclones in the northern Atlantic and on both sides of the equator in the Pacific, but never in the southern Atlantic – until 2004. On 28 March 2004, Hurricane Catarina slammed into Brazil, suggesting that recent weather patterns are starkly different from those of the 20th century.

What is going on? Are these freak occurrences or signs of something bigger?

In 2008, Kerry Emanuel again sought answers to these questions. This time, however, the team of scientists he led used a completely different approach. Instead of using historical records, they worked with Global Circulation Models that scientists around the world now use to forecast the effects of climate change under different conditions. The models, says Emanuel, do not explain the real world pattern perfectly, but they do show one thing without a doubt: 'The idea that there is no connection between hurricanes and global warming, that's not supported' (Emanuel et al, 2008).

While there is no level of data or anecdote that that will satisfy hardened sceptics, many scientists now believe, like Emanuel, that the increasing intensity of storms over the Atlantic is merely a symptom of a bigger problem: global climate change. As the Earth's average temperature grows warmer, they say, atmospheric and oceanic patterns are beginning to shift, fuelling increased storms and unusual weather events.

Temperatures at the planet's surface increased by an estimated 1.4 degrees Fahrenheit (°F) (0.8 degrees Celsius (°C)) between 1900 and 2005. The past decade was the hottest on record during the last 150 years, with 2005 being the warmest year on record during that time (NASA, 2007).

Again, sceptics argue that this is part of the natural variability in the Earth's temperature, but the majority of scientists now agree that it is more likely due to increased concentrations of heat-trapping greenhouse gases (GHGs) in the atmosphere. The US National Oceanic and Atmospheric Administration (NOAA) reported that carbon dioxide (CO_2), the most common GHG, is increasing at ever faster rates. Between 1970 and 2000, CO_2 concentrations rose at an average annual rate of 1.5 parts per million (ppm). That average has ticked upward to 2.1ppm since 2000, and in 2007 the mean growth rate was 2.14ppm. Atmospheric CO_2 levels are now higher than they have been for at least the last 650,000 years (NOAA, 2008).

Box 1.1 A look at the science

Prior to the industrial revolution of the 18th and 19th centuries, the atmospheric concentration of CO_2 was approximately 280 parts per million (ppm). Today, the atmospheric concentration of CO_2 has risen to 387 ppm (NOAA, 2008), largely because of anthropogenic emissions from the burning of fossil fuels used in transportation, agriculture, energy generation and the production of everyday materials. The loss of natural carbon sinks (places where carbon is pulled out of the atmosphere and trapped either in geological formations or in biological organisms) – on land and in the ocean – is also contributing to increased levels of CO_2 in the atmosphere.

The rapid rise in concentration of CO_2 in the atmosphere concerns scientists because CO_2 is a greenhouse gas. GHGs allow sunlight to enter the atmosphere, but they keep the heat released from the Earth's surface from getting back out.

While recent trends show a gradual warming trend of the Earth's surface, some scientists fear future climate change will not be linear. 'The Earth's system', says Wallace Broecker, Newberry Professor of Earth and Environmental Sciences at Columbia University, 'has sort of proven that if it's given small nudges, it can take large leaps. By tripling the amount of carbon dioxide in the atmosphere, we are giving the system a huge nudge' (Hawn, 2004).

The 'large leaps' to which Broecker refers are better known as 'abrupt climate changes' in the world of science. Over the course of thousands of years, such changes have left geological records of themselves in ice cores and stalagmites. These records show that past temperature swings on our planet have been as large as 18°F (7.8°C) and have occurred over time scales as short as two years.

Using the analogy of a car moving along an unknown road at night, Klaus Lackner, a geophysicist at Columbia University, argues that our incomplete

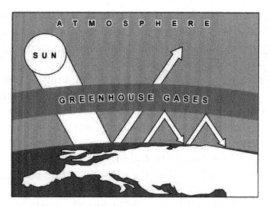

Figure 1.1 *The greenhouse effect*
Source: Pew Center on Global Climate Change, 2001

understanding of the natural system is no excuse for delaying action: 'We sort of vaguely see in the headlights a sharp turn. There are two possibilities.

You can say: "I'm going to ignore that and keep going at 90 miles an hour because you cannot prove to me that the curve is not banked and therefore I might make it" ... or you can put on the brakes' (Hawn, 2004).

Noting that there could be an oil slick and no bank to the road, Lackner says the good news is that we have the technology to put on the brakes. He adds, however, that if we want to stabilize the amount of CO_2 in the atmosphere at double the natural level (roughly 500ppm, which still might leave us with an ice-free Arctic Ocean), we have to start now (Hawn, 2004). The most recent report from the Intergovernmental Panel on Climate Change (IPCC) concluded that 'greenhouse gas emissions at or above current rates would cause further warming and induce many changes in the global climate system during the 21st century that would very likely be larger than those observed during the 20th century' (IPCC, 2007).

Market theory

To start towards stabilized levels of atmospheric CO_2, climate policy makers argue that we not only need to prime the research pump behind clean energy technologies and emission reductions strategies; we must also generate the market pull for them.

Enter the global carbon market. Many think markets for emissions reductions are among the most innovative and cost-effective means society has of creating a market pull for new clean energy technologies while, at the same time, putting a price on pollution and thereby providing incentives for people to emit less.

The theory is that carbon markets are able to achieve this magic because they help channel resources towards the most cost-effective means of reducing greenhouse gas emissions. At the same time, they punish (monetarily) those who emit more than an established quota, and reward (again, monetarily) those who emit less. In so doing, they encourage people to emit less and change the economics of energy technologies, making technologies that emit less carbon more competitive vis-à-vis their carbon-intensive counterparts.

There is other magic at work as well. By turning units of pollution into units of property, the system makes it possible to exchange pollution from Cape Town with pollution from Cape Cod. If business managers find reducing their company's emissions too costly, they can buy excess reductions from a facility where reductions are less expensive. The bigger the market, the theory goes, the greater the likelihood that efficiencies will be found.

By aggregating information about the value of carbon allowances, the market is sending signals to potential polluters. In a world where pollution has no price, the default decision will always be to pollute, but in a world where pollution has a financial cost, the decision is no longer easy. In today's European emissions market, for instance, emitting 1 tonne of CO_2 has in the past cost polluters anywhere from €7.02 up to €32.85. Polluters suddenly must consider a new suite of options: do they accept the cost of added pollution, change fuel mixes or simply conserve energy?

Once markets take shape, emitters have a variety of options available to them. If they believe they can reduce emissions cheaply by changing production processes or experimenting with new technologies, they have an incentive to do so. If they believe they can change their production process, but that this will take time, emitters can purchase credits up front in the hope that they will be able to make them back through the use of emission reductions technologies down the line. If, on the other hand, emitters believe they will emit more in the long run, they can buy credits now (or options on credits once secondary markets develop) for use later. In short, the system enables the trading of emissions across temporal as well as geographic boundaries – a basic benefit of markets.

The market-based approach also allows other, third party players such as speculators to enter the fray. By agreeing to take on market risks in exchange for possible paybacks, speculators assume the risks that others are either unwilling or unable to shoulder. Other interested parties in addition to speculators can also get involved. If, for example, an environmental group wants to see emissions decrease below a regulated target, they can raise money to buy and retire emissions allowances. This drives up the cost of emissions and can force utilities to become more efficient.

It is, of course, important to note that some people dispute the net gain of this approach, and others feel that markets allow companies to 'greenwash' previously tarnished environmental reputations without changing their behaviour in important ways. 'Carbon offsets are based on fictitious carbon accounting, and can by themselves not make a company carbon neutral,' argues Larry Lohmann of The Corner House, a UK-based non-governmental organization (NGO). 'The practice of offsetting is slowing down innovation at home and abroad and diverting attention away from the root causes of climate change' (Wright, 2006).

This debate notwithstanding, experimentation with environmental markets is now widespread. Ever since the US established the first large-scale environmental market (to regulate emissions of gases that lead to acid rain) in 1995, we have seen environmental markets emerging in everything from wetlands to woodpeckers.

Carbon markets

The term 'carbon market' refers to the buying and selling of emissions credits that have been either distributed by a regulatory body or generated by GHG emissions reductions projects, respectively. Six GHGs are generally included in 'carbon' markets: carbon dioxide, methane, nitrous oxide, sulphur hexafluoride, hydrofluorocarbons and perfluorocarbons.

GHG emissions reductions are traded in the form of carbon credits, which represent the reduction of GHGs equal to 1 metric ton (tonne) of carbon dioxide equivalent (tCO_2e), the most common GHG. A group of scientists associated with the IPCC has determined the global warming potential (GWP) of each gas in terms of its equivalent in tonnes of carbon dioxide (tCO_2e) over the course of 100 years. For example, the GHG methane has a GWP roughly 23 times greater than CO_2, hence 1 tonne of methane equals about 23 tCO_2e. Likewise, other gases have different equivalences in terms of tCO_2e, with some of them (perfluorocarbons) worth thousands of tonnes of CO_2e.

Carbon credits can be accrued through two different types of transactions. In project-based transactions, emissions credits are the result of emissions reductions achieved by a specific carbon offset project. Allowance-based transactions involve the trading of issued allowances (also known as permits) created and allocated by regulators under a cap-and-trade regime. In cap-and-trade, the regulatory authority caps the quantity of emissions that participants are permitted to emit and issues a number of tradable allowance units equal to the cap. Participants who reduce their emissions internally beyond required levels can sell unused allowances to other participants at whatever price the market will bear. Likewise, participants who exceed their required levels can purchase extra allowances from participants who outperformed their emissions targets.

The global carbon market can be separated into two sub-markets: the compliance (or regulatory) and voluntary markets. Because the voluntary market inherently does not operate under a universal cap, all carbon credits purchased in the voluntary market are project-based transactions (with the exception of those traded on the Chicago Climate Exchange).

Compliance carbon markets

There are now a number of compliance (regulated) cap-and-trade carbon markets around the world, and most are underpinned in one way or another by the Kyoto Protocol.

Currently ratified by 182 countries, the Protocol is a legally binding treaty committing industrialized countries to reducing their collective GHGs 5.2 per cent below 1990 levels by 2012. The Kyoto Protocol's authors created three

Box 1.2 The Chicago Climate Exchange (CCX)

Richard Sandor, a former chief economist at the Chicago Board of Trade, launched 'North America's only voluntary, legally binding rules-based greenhouse gas emission reductions and trading system' in 2003 (www.chicagoclimatex.com). He called the trading platform the Chicago Climate Exchange (CCX).

The Exchange refers to the carbon credits it trades as carbon financial instruments (CFIs, also measured in tCO_2e) and restricts trading to members who have voluntarily signed up to its mandatory reductions policy. During the pilot phase (2003–2006) members agreed to reduce greenhouse gas emissions 1 per cent per year from a baseline determined by their average emissions during the period 1998 to 2001 (see www.chicagoclimatex.com). The current goal (Phase II) is for members to reduce their total emissions by 6 per cent below the baseline by 2010.

Like the carbon market in general, CCX trades six different types of GHGs denominated in terms of tCO_2e. The majority of trading on CCX is allowance-based, rather than project-based. In other words, CCX operates as a cap-and-trade system in which members agree to cap emissions at a stated level and then trade allowances with other participants when they are either under or over their target. While CCX allows members to purchase offsets as a means of meeting emissions targets, offsets registered on the Exchange have accounted for just 10 per cent of total verified emission reductions (CCX, 2007).

When and where offset projects are used, CCX requires that an approved third party organization verifies the project's emission reductions and that they meet standards set by the Exchange.

Since its launch in late 2003, CCX has grown in membership from 19 institutions to over 350 institutions. Ford Motor, International Paper, IBM, American Electric Power, the City of Chicago, the State of New Mexico, the World Resources Institute and Natural Capitalism Inc are just a few of its members from the business, governmental and philanthropic sectors. In 2007, CCX traded 23 million tCO_2e for a total value of US$72 million (up from 1.45 million tCO_2e traded in 2005 worth US$2.7 million). Total market value through the first quarter of 2008 was already at US$81 million, suggesting the market is still growing quickly year-on-year (Hamilton et al, 2008).

In 2005, CCX created the European Carbon Exchange (ECX), a wholly owned subsidiary, which has since become the largest exchange trading carbon credits in the EU Emission Trading Scheme (see below). CCX also announced the creation of three new exchanges in 2006: the Montreal Climate Exchange (MCeX), the Northeastern Climate Exchange (NECX) and the New York Climate Exchange (NYCX). These initiatives are designed to interface with carbon credit schemes in Canada and with the Regional Greenhouse Gas Initiative (RGGI) in the US northeast. Since 2006, CCX, ECX and MCeX have been owned by Climate Exchange Plc, a publicly traded company listed on the AIM of the London Stock Exchange. The first trade on the Montreal Climate Exchange took place in May 2008, launching Canada's first carbon trading market.

major 'flexibility mechanisms' in order to provide the treaty's signatories with a cost-effective means of achieving their GHG emission reductions targets. These mechanisms are the basis for the regulated international compliance carbon market, and they are:

- *Emissions trading:* An allowance-based transaction system that enables countries with emissions targets to purchase carbon credits from one another in order to fulfil their Kyoto commitments.
- *Joint Implementation (JI):* A project-based transaction system that allows developed countries to purchase carbon credits from GHG reduction projects implemented in another developed country or in a country with an economy in transition (specifically countries of the former Soviet Union). Credits from JI projects are referred to as Emission Reduction Units (ERUs).
- *Clean Development Mechanism (CDM):* Another project-based transaction system through which industrialized countries can accrue carbon credits by financing carbon reduction projects in developing countries. Carbon offsets originating from registered and approved CDM projects are known as Certified Emissions Reductions (CERs).

The World Bank estimates that in 2007, buyers contracted for 551 million tonnes (Mt) of CO_2e in the primary CDM market of the Kyoto Protocol. Analysts put the total value of the CDM market (primary and secondary) in 2007 at over US$12 billion. The JI market of the Kyoto Protocol is believed to have traded only 41Mt of carbon and to have been worth around US$499 million the same year (Capoor and Ambrosi, 2008).

To meet their Kyoto obligations, countries have established (or are establishing) national or regional emissions trading. In January 2005, for instance, the European Union launched the first phase of the EU Emission Trading Scheme (EU ETS) to help achieve the GHG emission reductions targets required by the Kyoto Protocol. The EU ETS involves all of the EU's member states and allows limited trading via the three Kyoto mechanisms described above through a linking directive. More specifically, EU members may trade allowances (known as EU emissions allowances, or EUAs) with one another, or they may buy and sell carbon credits – ERUs and CERs – generated by JI or CDM projects.

By the end of its first year of trading, the EU ETS had transacted an estimated 362 million tonnes (Mt) of carbon credits, worth approximately €7.2 billion (or US$9 billion) (Capoor and Ambrosi, 2006; Point Carbon, 2006). It has been estimated that the global carbon market traded nearly 5 billion tonnes of carbon credits in 2008 and was worth €92 billion (Point Carbon, 2009).

Outside of Europe, regulated emissions trading schemes related to the Kyoto Protocol have not developed as quickly. For instance, Japan and Canada have both ratified the treaty, and Japanese companies, in particular, have been active buyers of carbon credits on the CDM market, but as of the date of publication of this book, neither country has launched a national, regulated emissions trading scheme of its own. The Japanese government has a government-mediated

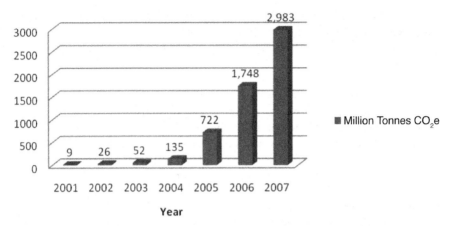

Figure 1.2   *Growth in trading volume, global carbon markets*
Note: The launch of the European Union's Emission Trading Scheme in 2005 drove huge expansion in the global carbon market that year (Capoor and Ambrosi, 2006; Capoor and Ambrosi, 2008; Hamilton et al, 2008).

voluntary market for carbon and is in the process of setting up a national scheme, as is New Zealand, while the Canadian government has indicated that it is not likely to meet its Kyoto targets and has talked of scrapping plans for a national emissions trading scheme altogether. At the same time, several Canadian provinces have opted into the Western Climate Initiative (WCI), a regional trading programme with western US states set to begin trading in 2010, and one Canadian province, Alberta, has launched its own trading scheme.

The explosive growth of the global compliance carbon market under the Kyoto Protocol has meant that prices for carbon credits have been extremely volatile, with carbon trading anywhere from €7 to €32 a tonne (Point Carbon, 2006). Despite this volatility, carbon markets around the world have matured, and in 2008 the global carbon market was valued at a whopping US$64 billion (€47 billion) (Capoor and Ambrosi, 2008).

As regulators and participants refine their approaches to allocating and trading carbon credits, new investment vehicles and emission reductions strategies are emerging. The World Bank estimated that the total capitalization of carbon investment vehicles could top US$13 billion in 2008 (Capoor and Ambrosi, 2008).

A short section from the World Bank's *State and Trends of the Carbon Market 2008* report suggests the level of sophistication to which the compliance carbon market has evolved and matured:

> *Financial institutions have entered the carbon world acquiring pioneering carbon aggregators and building a base for origination of carbon assets globally. An increasing number of carbon contracts and carbon-based derivatives are becoming available. Specialized companies and institutions have sprung up to service several aspects of the carbon value chain; some have begun to pair carbon finance with more traditional skills found in other commodity markets.*

Several dedicated funds focusing on developing and participating in greenfield projects have been launched (i.e., these funds are either partially replenished with carbon revenue streams or account with the sale of the credits to meet investor expectations of return). Large international banks have established structured origination teams to pick up principal positions in carbon-rich projects and have set up carbon trading desks, seeking arbitrage opportunities. Financial institutions offer products that reduce or transfer risk, for instance by offering delivery guarantees for carbon assets in the secondary market.

Echoing the World Bank's analyses over the years, Annie Petsonk, International Counsel for Environmental Defense's Global and Regional Air Program, says she is particularly pleased with some of the innovations triggered by the CDM. Petsonk says individuals and institutions, inspired by the active market in Europe, are now pouring money into new clean technologies in the hope of capitalizing on a perceived first-mover advantage. Indeed, the European experience with carbon trading suggests that large-scale environmental markets are not only feasible, but are also capable of changing the way businesses relate to environmental issues (Kenny, 2006).

Challenges remain, however, and the first half of 2008 has seen a growing spread between EU allowances and CERs from the CDM, driven largely by uncertainty over the future of the CDM market in a post-2012 international climate change agreement (Capoor and Ambrosi, 2008).

Movement in the US

The US did not ratify the Kyoto Protocol, and the US federal government does not currently regulate CO_2 or any other GHGs regulated under Kyoto as climate change-related pollutants. Having ratified the Montreal Protocol, the US does regulate ozone-depleting GHGs, such as chlorofluorocarbons (CFCs), which are being phased out entirely on the international scale.

To compensate for the lack of national CO_2 regulation, roughly two dozen states have initiated their own regulations alone or in conjunction with others. Legislation is quickly evolving at the national and multi-state levels as more states step up to the plate on climate legislation and members of Congress announce new legislative proposals on a monthly basis. As of March 2008, legislators in the 110th US Congress introduced more than 195 bills, resolutions and amendments addressing climate change (Pew Center on Global Climate Change, 2008). Currently, GHG emissions markets exist or may soon exist under the following regimes:

Oregon Standard: In 1997, Oregon enacted the Oregon Standard, the first regulation of CO_2 in the US. The Oregon Standard requires that new power plants built in Oregon reduce their CO_2 emissions to a level 17 per cent below those of the most efficient combined cycle plants, either through direct reduction or offsets. Plants may propose specific offset projects or pay mitigation funds to The Climate Trust, a non-profit created by law to implement projects that avoid, sequester or displace CO_2 emissions (The Climate Trust, 2008).

Regional Greenhouse Gas Initiative (RGGI): On the East Coast, ten states (Connecticut, Delaware, Maryland, Massachusetts, Maine, New Hampshire, New Jersey, New York, Rhode Island and Vermont) have developed the Regional Greenhouse Gas Initiative (RGGI), a regional strategy to reduce CO_2 emissions utilizing a cap-and-trade system. Although RGGI will not officially launch until January 2009, the first auction of emission permits took place in September 2008. The ten states' allowances represent approximately $171MtCO_2e$ per year. The emissions cap applies initially to power plants in member states that use fossil fuels to generate over half their electricity and have energy production capacities above 25MW. The cap's applicability is much broader for power plants that commenced operations after 2004, and includes power plants with fossil fuels constituting over 5 per cent of their annual total heat input (RGGI, 2007). The programme may be extended to include other GHGs in the future. Member states have agreed to allocate the revenues of at least 25 per cent of allowances to consumer benefit programmes. States maintain autonomy over allocating the remaining 75 per cent of allowances (RGGI, 2007). RGGI has a sliding scale that permits the use of offsets based on market prices: the lower the price of allowances, the more restrictive the use of offsets.

California's Global Warming Solutions Act (AB 32): The first state-wide legislation in the US to cap all GHG emissions from major industries and to include penalties for non-compliance. Under the Act, California's State Air Resources Board (CARB) is required to create, monitor and enforce a GHG emissions reporting and reduction programme. The California Market Advisory Committee (MAC) was created in December 2006 to provide recommendations on the implementation of the Act. In the implementation of AB 32, Governor Schwarzenegger authorized CARB to establish market-based compliance mechanisms to achieve reduction goals. The MAC's current recommendations include: the eventual incorporation of all GHG-emitting sectors of the economy into the cap-and-trade system; a first-seller approach whereby responsibility is assigned to the utility that initially sells electricity into the state; an allocation design that combines free and auctioned pollution permits, with the amount being auctioned increasing over time; and the promotion of linkages with other emerging cap-and-trade systems (CalEPA, 2007).

The Western Climate Initiative (WCI): An emerging regional trading market that currently includes seven US states (California, New Mexico, Oregon, Washington, Arizona, Utah and Montana) as well as four Canadian provinces (British Columbia, Manitoba, Quebec and Ontario). It was formed in February 2007, and member states have committed to a 15 per cent GHG emission reductions goal below a 2005 baseline by 2020. The WCI plans to begin mandatory measuring and monitoring of emissions in 2010 for all regulated entities, reporting of emissions in early 2011, and to launch a cap-and-trade scheme in 2012.

Midwestern Regional GHG Program: This regional cap-and-trade programme is less developed than the others but is aiming for an emissions reduction target greater than that of the WCI. The Program currently consists of the following members: Iowa, Illinois, Kansas, Minnesota, Wisconsin, Michigan and Manitoba (Canada). The Midwestern Greenhouse Gas Accord was signed in November 2007 and aims to incorporate an approximate emissions target of 16 per cent below 2005 levels. The programme is scheduled to start in 2012 and will incorporate a regional cap-and-trade system covering most sectors of the economy. The scheme aims to cover approximately $1107MtCO_2e$ per year by 2012 (Hamilton et al, 2008).

Australia's pioneers

While Europe's compliance carbon market leads the world in terms of sophistication and scale, it is worth noting that the state of New South Wales (NSW) in Australia launched the NSW Greenhouse Gas Abatement Scheme on 1 January 2003, two years before the first trade ever took place on the EU ETS.

The NSW Greenhouse Gas Reduction Scheme (GGAS) is a mandatory, state-level cap-and-trade programme designed to reduce GHG emissions associated with the production and use of electricity, and to develop and encourage activities to offset the production of GHGs. Legislators set the target at 8.65 tonnes of CO_2 equivalent per capita in 2003, decreasing by about 3 per cent each year through 2007, when it became and will remain at 7.27 tonnes. It requires individual electricity retailers and certain other parties who buy or sell electricity in NSW to meet mandatory benchmarks based on the size of their shares of the electricity market.

If a regulated emitter exceeds its target, it has the choice of either paying a penalty of AU$11.50 (about US$9) per tCO_2e or purchasing New South Wales Greenhouse Abatement Certificates (NGACs). NGACs can be generated by approved providers with projects in the state that lead to low-emissions electricity generation, improved energy efficiency, biological CO_2 sequestration, or reduced on site emissions not directly related to electricity consumption. The initiative does not accept credits, such as CERs or ERUs, from outside of the state. The NSW GGAS traded some 25 million certificates in 2007 for a total market value of US$224 million (€164 million).

According to the World Bank, outside of the Kyoto markets, the NSW GGAS is the world's largest regulated cap-and-trade GHG market, with about $25MtCO_2e$ traded in 2007 and an estimated value of US$224 million (Capoor and Ambrosi, 2008). After years of holding out, Australia ratified the Kyoto Protocol in 2007, soon after the inauguration of new Prime Minster Kevin Rudd. According to the current government, a national emissions trading scheme will be launched in Australia no later than 2010 (Capoor and Ambrosi, 2008).

Unfortunately, the emissions reductions driven by current state and regional schemes in Australia and the US are tiny compared to those mandated by the Kyoto Protocol, and the emission reductions driven by the Kyoto Protocol are tiny compared to those scientists deem necessary. Throw in other non-market-based reduction strategies around the world and Mark Kenber, head of policy strategy at The Climate Group in London, says, 'The policies that we see around the world are nowhere near what the science suggests we need.'

Thin end of the wedge

Guy Brasseur, head of the Hamburg-based Max Planck Institute for Meteorology, echoed Kenber's comments when he told the European Parliament in November of 2005, 'Kyoto won't be enough.'

'Emissions', said Brasseur, 'will need to fall by 80 or 90 per cent, rather than 5 or 10 per cent, to have an effect on the models. In terms of a response, Kyoto is only a start' (Kenny, 2006).

In the absence of a much larger global effort to reduce GHG emissions, models suggest the amount of CO_2 trapped in the atmosphere will double within the next 50 years and quadruple by the turn of the century. According to Professor Steve Pacala, head of Princeton University's Carbon Mitigation Initiative, that would 'bring out the monsters behind the door' – melting the Greenland ice cap, washing away coastal cities, spreading famine, and intermixing hurricanes with prolonged droughts (Kenny, 2006).

While scientists cannot say how many gigatonnes of CO_2 emitted into the atmosphere will produce how many degrees of warming, they do agree that roughly 7 billion tonnes – 7 gigatonnes – of CO_2 emissions must be prevented from entering the atmosphere during the next 50 years in order to stabilize the concentration in the atmosphere at 500ppm. Pacala slices a metaphorical emissions pie into seven wedges in order to demonstrate how the world might achieve a 7-gigatonne cut (Pacala and Socolow, 2004). With each wedge representing 1 gigatonne of CO_2 emissions, Western Europe's emissions comprise about one-seventh of the pie. In other words, if the ETS meets its current targets and then extends them for the next four decades, it would remove only one wedge of the pie (Kenny, 2006).

The current carbon market, it seems, represents only the very thin end of the wedge when it comes to combating climate change. Fortunately, however, wedges sometimes work like levers. Recognizing the need for increased action, some institutions and individuals have undertaken voluntary commitments to minimize (or even neutralize) their contribution to climate change by offsetting their emissions through investments in projects that either remove an equivalent amount of CO_2 from the atmosphere, or prevent it from being emitted in the first place. Hundreds of companies – ranging from Google to General Electric – have now incorporated the idea of carbon offsetting into corporate sustainability plans, spawning a global voluntary market worth an estimated $331 million in 2007 (Hamilton et al, 2008).

Much like the credits traded in a regulated cap-and-trade scheme, voluntary offset projects generate credits equal to the removal or avoided emission of 1 tonne of CO_2. Institutions voluntarily purchasing credits either have set caps on themselves, such as a 10 per cent reduction below 1990 levels, or have decided to offset some or all of the emissions related to their activities. Institutions claiming to have offset their GHG emissions must retire credits purchased. As in a compliance market, carbon credits in a voluntary market ideally allow actors to reduce emissions at least cost.

Voluntary carbon markets

Voluntary carbon markets are nothing new; in fact, they pre-date all regulated carbon markets. The world's first carbon offset deal was brokered in 1989 (long before the Kyoto Protocol was signed, let alone ratified), when AES Corp, an American electricity company, invested in an agroforestry project in Guatemala (Hawn, 2005).

Since trees use and store carbon as they grow (an example of carbon sequestration), AES reasoned it could offset the GHGs it emitted during electricity production by paying farmers in Guatemala to plant 50 million pine and eucalyptus trees on their land (Hawn, 2005). AES, like other companies since, hoped to reduce its 'carbon footprint' for philanthropic and marketing reasons, not because it was forced to do so by legislation or global treaty. The deal thus was voluntary, marking the beginning of a voluntary carbon market that remains as controversial and interesting today as it was in 1989.

Unlike the regulated markets, the voluntary markets do not rely on legally mandated reductions to generate demand. As a result, they sometimes suffer from fragmentation and a lack of widely available impartial information. The fragmented and opaque nature of the voluntary markets can, in large part, be attributed to the fact that they are composed of deals that are negotiated on a case-by-case basis, and that many of these deals require neither that the carbon credits undergo a uniform certification or verification process nor registration with any central body. As a result, there are almost as many types of carbon transactions on the voluntary markets as there are buyers and sellers; a variety of businesses and non-profits based on different models sell a range of products, certified to a wide array of standards.

The lack of uniformity, transparency and registration in the voluntary markets has won them a great deal of criticism from some environmentalists who claim that they are a game of smoke and mirrors rather than an engine of actual environmental progress. Many buyers also say they are wary of the voluntary carbon markets because transactions often carry real risks of non-delivery. Some companies buying carbon credits also fear that they will be criticized in the media if the carbon they are buying isn't seen to meet the highest possible standards.

Of concern to environmentalists and buyers alike is the fact that the voluntary carbon markets' lack of regulation may mean they cannot reach the scale necessary to impact the problem. Because they lack a regulatory driver, demand for credits can be volatile and fickle. The sudden explosion of the Kyoto-driven carbon markets in 2005 shows the difference that regulation can make in growing a carbon market. Clearly, regulation is key to driving large-scale demand. 'The voluntary credit market could grow by an order of magnitude or two orders of magnitude and it's still not going to impact the problem,' explains Mark Trexler, Director of EcoSecurities Global Consulting Services (Trexler et al, 2006).

Despite the shortcomings of the voluntary markets, many feel they are fast-evolving arenas with some distinct and important advantages over the regulated carbon markets. For example, while the wide range of products emerging from the voluntary markets can be confusing to potential buyers, these products can also be highly innovative and less expensive. Numerous suppliers say they benefit from this flexibility and the lower transaction costs associated with it.

For example, getting a carbon offset project approved by the CDM Executive Board under the Kyoto Protocol costs up to US$350,000 (Kollmuss et al, 2008). By the time the United Nations CDM Executive Board finally registers a typical small-scale CDM project (essentially creating the CER that can be sold on the CDM markets), the United Nations Development Programme (UNDP) calculates that the project's total up-front costs will account for 14–22 per cent of the net present value of its revenue from carbon credits (Krolik, 2006). For many projects, coming up with the start-up capital to prepare a project for the compliance carbon market is prohibitively difficult.

The voluntary carbon markets, on the other hand, don't have these sorts of transaction costs (at least, not at the moment). They can avoid 'bottlenecks' in the CDM methodology approval process and obtain carbon financing for methodologies that aren't currently 'approved' by the CDM Executive Board. For example, the Nature Conservancy is working towards obtaining carbon financing for forest protection projects (which in Kyoto parlance is referred to as 'avoided deforestation'), a concept not currently approved to produce carbon credits under the CDM process.

The innovation, flexibility and lower transaction costs of the voluntary carbon markets can benefit buyers as well as suppliers. Creativity, speed, cost-effectiveness and the ability to support specific types of projects (e.g. those that also benefit local communities or biodiversity) can often be clear and valuable benefits for an organization purchasing carbon offsets to meet a public relations or branding need.

Having weighed such pros and cons, many non-profit organizations are supportive of the voluntary carbon markets because they provide individuals – not just corporations and large organizations – with a means of participating in the fight against climate change in a way that the compliance markets do not. In particular, some environmentalists view the voluntary carbon markets as an important tool for educating the public about climate change and their potential role in addressing the problem. Some sellers and buyers of carbon credits prefer the voluntary carbon markets precisely because they do not depend on regulation.

In 2007, a range of articles in the mainstream press highlighted various issues related to offset quality (in particular, the importance of additionality) in the voluntary carbon markets. In response, suppliers embraced a range of tools for producing high quality credits and proving their legitimacy – notably standards and registries, which are discussed in more detail in Chapter 2. As the international political community struggles to implement an effective climate change framework, these infrastructural developments, coupled with the tremendous growth in the voluntary carbon markets over the last several years, indicate that the voluntary carbon markets have the potential to become an active driver of change today – not ten years from now.

A more formal affair

Be they fans or critics, experts agree that the voluntary carbon markets are in a unique period. Spurred by the success of the regulated carbon markets, the voluntary markets are formalizing, as investors who cut their teeth on the regulated markets look for other places to put their money, and as buyers and sellers consolidate around a few guiding practices and business models from which conclusions can be drawn about market direction and opportunities.

Although nobody has exact numbers on the size of the global voluntary carbon market, most think it has grown rapidly in the last two years. In their *State of the Voluntary Carbon Markets 2008* report, Ecosystem Marketplace and New Carbon Finance were able to track the following transaction volumes presented in Table 1.1 (below), though the actual number of transactions is likely to be significantly greater.

Table 1.1 *Size of the voluntary carbon markets*

Year	Voluntary markets' volume (millions tonnes/yr)
Pre-2002	38
2002	10
2003	5
2004	11
2005	11
2006	25
2007	65

Source: Ecosystem Marketplace / New Carbon Finance, 2008

While maturing quickly, the voluntary markets remain small, transacting around 2 per cent of the volume of the Kyoto markets in 2007 (Hamilton et al, 2008). Despite the comparatively small scale of the voluntary carbon markets, some investors believe they are poised for explosive growth, and many companies see real business opportunities associated with the creation of carbon neutral products for retail consumption. If these predictions are to be borne out, most market players think it will be necessary to formalize and streamline the voluntary markets, making them more accessible and gaining the confidence of large institutional buyers in Australia, Europe, Asia and North America.

At present there are several related and unrelated efforts underway to make the voluntary carbon markets more 'investor-friendly' by creating registries, documenting the size of the markets and standardizing the credits being sold. In the past two years, the standards and registry infrastructure has matured rapidly. Where third party verification was non-existent or hardly utilized by project developers a couple of years ago, verification standards have become a 'must-do' for many retailers and developers seeking to sell high quality offsets. As of late 2008, more than a dozen standards had emerged to verify or provide guidelines for offset project development in the voluntary markets.

Building on the establishment of standards, a new feature of the voluntary carbon market infrastructure is sprouting up across the globe: carbon credit registries. These registries are designed to track credit transactions and ownership as well as reduce the risk that a single credit can be sold to more than one buyer. When dealing with a commodity as intangible as a carbon credit, such registries are crucial, but they had not been prevalent in the voluntary markets until recently. Several new registries were launched during the first four months of 2008 alone, including the New Zealand-based registry and exchange TZ1, the California Climate Action Registry's Climate Action Reserve, and The Gold Standard's Registry for VERs (the latter two set up by market infrastructure provider APX).

Whatever one's take on the long-term prospects of the voluntary carbon markets, it seems clear that in the short term, the markets are evolving quickly, creating new economic and environmental opportunities for investors, businesses, non-profits and individuals. It is therefore important to understand how the voluntary markets operate. In the next chapter, then, we will turn our attention to addressing a basic but all-important question: how do the voluntary carbon markets really work?

References

California Environmental Protection Agency (CalEPA) (2007) 'Expert advisors release final cap-and-trade report: Recommendations intended to complement California's ongoing efforts to reduce emissions', www.climatechange.ca.gov/notices/news/2007-06-29_MAC_FINAL_RELEASE.PDF

Capoor, K. and Ambrosi, P. (2006) *State and Trends of the Carbon Market 2006*, The World Bank, Washington DC

Capoor, K. and Ambrosi, P. (2008) *State and Trends of the Carbon Market 2008*, The World Bank, Washington DC

Chicago Climate Exchange (CCX) (2007) 'Overview and frequently asked questions: Project-based credits – 'offsets' – in the Chicago Climate Exchange', available online at www.chicagoclimatex.com/docs/offsets/General_Offsets_faq.pdf

Emanuel, K. A. (2005) 'Increasing destructiveness of tropical cyclones over the past 30 years', *Nature*, vol 436, pp686–688

Emanuel, K., Sundararajan, R. and Williams, J. (2008) 'Hurricanes and global warming: Results from downscaling IPCC AR4 simulations', *Bulletin of American Meteorological Society*, vol 89, pp347–367

Hamilton, K. (2006) 'Navigating a nebula: Institutional use of the U.S. voluntary carbon market', unpublished Masters thesis at the Yale School of Forestry

Hamilton, K., Sjardin, M., Marcello, T. and Xu, G. (2008) 'Forging a frontier: State of the voluntary carbon markets 2008', The Ecosystem Marketplace and New Carbon Finance, May

Hawn, A. (2004) *Don't Wait Until 'Day After Tomorrow' to Solve Fossil Fuel Emissions Problem*, St Paul Pioneer Press, St Paul, Minnesota

Hawn, A. (2005) 'Horses for courses: Voluntary vs. CDM carbon projects in Mexico', The Ecosystem Marketplace, www.ecosystemmarketplace.com

Intergovernmental Panel on Climate Change (IPCC) (2007) *Climate Change 2007: The Physical Science Basis: Summary for Policymakers*, IPCC Secretariat, Geneva, Switzerland

Kenny, A. (2006) 'The thin end of the wedge', The Ecosystem Marketplace, www.ecosystemmarketplace.com

Kollmuss, A., Zink, H. and Polycarp, C. (2008) *Making Sense of the Voluntary Carbon Market: A Comparison of Carbon Offset Standards*, World Wildlife Fund, Germany

Krolik, T. (2006) 'The Argentine Carbon Fund helps developers dance the dance', The Ecosystem Marketplace, www.ecosystemmarketplace.com

Lecocq, F. and Capoor, K. (2005) *State and Trends of the Carbon Market 2005*, The World Bank, Washington DC

NOAA (2008) 'Trends in atmospheric carbon dioxide – Mauna Loa', www.esrl.noaa.gov/gmd/ccgg/trends

Pacala, S. and Socolow, R. (2004) 'Stabilization wedges: Solving the climate problem for the next 50 years with current technologies', *Science*, vol 305, pp968–972

Pew Center on Global Climate Change (2001) 'The greenhouse effect', in Claussen, E. (ed) *Climate Change: Science, Strategies and Solutions*, Brill, Boston

Pew Center on Global Climate Change (2008) *Climate Action in Congress: US Climate Change Legislation*, www.pewclimate.org/what_s_being_done/in_the_congress

Point Carbon (2006) *Carbon 2006: Towards a Truly Global Market*, Hasselknippe, H. and Roine, K. (eds), www.pointcarbon.com/polopoly_fs/1.2843!Carbon_2006_final_print.pdf

Point Carbon (2009) '5.9 GT to trade globally in 2009–up 20% in volume–estimates Point Carbon', press release, 24 February

Regional Greenhouse Gas Initiative (RGGI) (2007) 'Overview of RGGI CO$_2$ budget trading program', www.rggi.org/docs/program_summary_10_07.pdf

The Climate Trust (2008) 'About us', www.climatetrust.org/programs_powerplant.php

Trexler, M., Walsh, M. and Kenber, M. (2006) Presentation at GreenT Forum: Raising the Bar for Voluntary Environmental Credit Markets, New York, 1–2 May

Wright, C. (2006) 'Carbon neutrality draws praise, raises expectations for HSBC', The Ecosystem Marketplace, www.ecosystemmarketplace.com

2

Understanding Supply and Demand in the Voluntary Carbon Markets

In December 2004, one of the world's largest banks – HSBC – surprised many observers by announcing it had decided to make its operations 'carbon neutral'. What surprised people wasn't so much that the bank had agreed to take the issue of climate change seriously, but that it had voluntarily agreed to spend millions of dollars over the next ten years to minimize its contribution to the problem. As a dry run, HSBC put out a tender for projects that would offset 170,000tCO$_2$e emitted by the bank during the last quarter of 2005. More than 100 emission reductions projects responded to HSBC's request, and the company was able to shortlist 17 based on criteria related to project volume, technology employed, country and vintage. When all was said and done, the company spent some US$750,000 buying offsets from a handful of projects in Germany, India, Australia and New Zealand (HSBC, 2005). But the process was a steep learning curve for the bank, which led environment adviser, Francis Sullivan to conclude: 'We need a better way of finding what we want in the market' (The Climate Group, 2005).

Over four years later, thousands of companies have declared themselves carbon neutral, and even entire countries have set timelines for carbon neutrality. Yet Sullivan's statement is still relevant to today's voluntary marketplace. It encapsulates both the challenges and opportunities in the voluntary carbon markets. Institutions buying and selling voluntary carbon offsets face a fragmented market, a complex supply chain and multiple, evolving standards. The range of 'climate neutral' product offerings increases every day, while carbon credit providers source offsets through an array of projects that range from planting trees in Australia to installing solar systems in Bangladeshi villages to capturing methane in American landfills. Hence, the market operates under the principle of *caveat emptor*: let the buyer beware. There are signs, however, that the voluntary markets have begun to mature. For instance, they have responded increasingly to consumer demand for quality assurance, as indicated by a significant rise in the share of third party certified offsets and registries to track ownership of emission reductions. This chapter attempts to help institutions assess these evolving opportunities by looking at the intricacies of supply and demand in the voluntary carbon markets.

A look at the supply chain

Institutions and individuals acquire offsets in a number of ways, but a simplified model of the voluntary carbon markets' supply chain typically includes the following elements: a project or project idea is generated, the resulting emission reductions are quantified and verified to some standard to create carbon credits, the credits are sold to intermediaries, and the intermediaries sell them on to businesses and individuals (Figure 2.1). Brokers and exchanges may assist in the distribution of offsets by facilitating transactions between buyers and sellers, but they usually do not buy or sell credits. In some cases, project developers may skip stage two and/or three of this sequence, selling either verified or unverified credits directly to consumers. The International Small Group and Tree Planting Alliance (TIST), for instance, sold verified offsets generated by subsistence farmers in East Africa and India directly to individual consumers via a virtual 'store' on eBay (Hawn, 2005). Likewise, The Nature Conservancy offers individuals the option of offsetting their carbon footprint via a donation that 'helps fund projects that produce measurable reductions in greenhouse gases'.

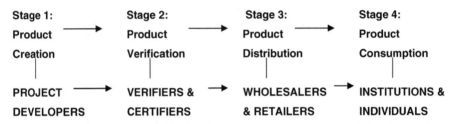

Figure 2.1 *Simplified supply chain of the voluntary carbon markets*

Stage 1: Product creation

In most cases, project development is the first step in the supply chain for carbon credits destined for the voluntary carbon markets. It is worth noting, however, that some projects start simply as a concept or idea and may not begin until a buyer supplies funding. In theory, a single landowner might develop a project on his or her land and sell the resulting offsets directly to a buyer. In practice, project developers include: non-profit organizations interested in combating climate change and/or contributing to sustainable development; private companies that generate emission reductions (e.g. timber companies) that are uniquely positioned to develop projects; small private sector companies that have been set up in response to the carbon market; or public sector agencies interested in 'seeding' the market. The bottom line, then, is that project developers come in all stripes and sizes.

Similarly, while the term *carbon credit* implies a uniform commodity, in reality carbon offsets originate from a wide variety of project types that differ at numerous levels. An exciting aspect of the voluntary market is that buyers can choose to provide carbon financing for specific types of projects and support specific co-benefits (e.g. benefits for biodiversity or benefits for local communities), in addition to greenhouse gas (GHG) reductions.

There is a range of differentiating factors between projects. A key difference is the type of project used to generate emission reductions. At the broadest level, offset projects can be categorized as those reducing GHG emissions at the source and those reducing GHG levels in the atmosphere through sequestration (see Table 2.1). For a more detailed description of the different kinds of offset projects and some of their respective advantages and disadvantages, see Appendix 1.

Table 2.1 *Project types generating carbon credits for the voluntary carbon markets*

Project group	Project type	Description	Co-benefits	Points to consider
I. Fossil fuel	*Energy efficiency*	Fossil fuel use is decreased by utilizing it more efficiently.	Cost savings; supports clean technology and reduces fossil fuel dependency and co-pollutants such as SOx, PM and VOCs.	If savings are greater than costs the need for carbon finance should be considered.
	Off-grid renewable energy and fuel switching	Fuel switching projects utilize fuels (such as many renewable energy sources) that provide energy with fewer emissions.	Reduction of other pollutants and reduced dependence on fossil fuels.	Supports clean technology.
II. Bio-carbon sequestration	*Reforestation/ afforestation of native tree species*	Carbon is sequestered in tree biomass and soi.l	Range of potential social and environmental benefits, such as biodiversity conservation, water filtration, erosion protection, etc.	Easy to communicate and tangible land restored. Measuring and monitoring is relatively complex Permanence and leakage risks.

Table 2.1   *Contd.*

Project group	Project type	Description	Co-benefits	Points to consider
II. Bio-carbon sequestration (contd.)	*Reforestation/ afforestation monoculture forestry*	Carbon is sequestered in tree biomass and soil.	Range of potential social and environmental benefits, such as water filtration, erosion protection, etc.	Easy to communicate and tangible land restored. Measuring and monitoring is relatively complex. Permanence and leakage risks. Potential concerns around environmental or social trade-offs. Potentially an extra income stream for sustainable timber harvesting.
	Avoided deforestation of native tree species	Conserving or changing forest management practices maintains carbon sequestration and avoids emissions released into the atmosphere.	Range of potential social and environmental benefits, such as biodiversity conservation, water filtration, erosion protection, etc.	Easy to communicate and tangible land conserved. Measuring and monitoring is relatively complex. Permanence and leakage risks. Not currently obtaining carbon finance under Kyoto markets.

Table 2.1 *Contd.*

Project group	Project type	Description	Co-benefits	Points to consider
II. Bio-carbon sequestration (contd.)	*Soil sequestration*	Carbon sequestered in soil is increased by farming practices such as no-till.	Numerous potential environmental benefits, such as reduced erosion and water pollution.	No-till often linked with GMO crops Significant permanence and financial additionality questions.
III. Bio-gas	*Methane capture and destruction from landfills*	Decomposing waste is covered by anaerobic digesters that cap and flare methane, which can also be used as a fuel source.	Somewhat reduced odours and risk of groundwater contamination.	Projects are easy to monitor and measure. In developed countries this project type is often required by law and hence additionality should be considered.
	Methane capture and destruction from livestock	Animal waste is covered by anaerobic digesters that cap and flare methane, which can also be used as a fuel source.	Reduced odours and risk of groundwater contamination.	Projects are easy to monitor and measure.
	Methane capture and destruction from coal mines	Instead of releasing underground methane via air vents, the gas is trapped and flared.	Potential safety benefits, especially in developing countries.	Projects are easy to monitor and measure. This project type is often required by law and hence additionality should be considered.

Table 2.1 *Contd.*

Project group	Project type	Description	Co-benefits	Points to consider
IV. Technological sequestration	*Geological sequestration*	CO_2 is injected into geologic formations, such as oil and gas reservoirs, coal seams, and deep saline reservoirs.	Few or none.	Precautionary principle uncertainties. Does not create incentives for reducing fossil fuel use.
	Industrial gas destruction	High global warming GHGs resulting from industrial processes are destroyed.	Few or none.	Very efficient means of reducing GHGs. There is some concern about perverse incentives and synchronicity; project start date should be carefully considered.
	Industrial gas reduction	Reduction of high global warming GHGs resulting from industrial processes (ex. aluminum production) via technology/efficiency improvements.	Few or none.	Very efficient means of reducing GHGs. There is some concern about perverse incentives and synchronicity; project start date should be carefully considered.

Another differentiating factor is project volume. Offsets available in the voluntary markets range from large-scale biodigester tanks that reduce methane emissions to small biogas stoves used in village huts. One advantage of the voluntary carbon markets over the regulated markets is that the voluntary markets may be able to provide the capital to enable smaller credit-generating operations (especially those in developing countries), which may be unable to bear the relatively high transaction costs per credit, to enter the regulated market.

Stage 2: Project validation and credit verification

The second stage in the supply chain, project validation and credit verification, begins the process of getting a product recognized by the market. While credits originating from Clean Development Mechanism (CDM) projects are referred to as Certified Emissions Reductions (CERs), offset credits in the voluntary market are often referred to as Verified (or Voluntary) Emission Reductions (VERs). This term – sometimes used as a de facto currency in the voluntary carbon markets – embodies the ideal of legitimate third party verification. Quantifying and verifying GHG emission reductions require significant technical expertise and monitoring throughout the project lifespan. Accounting questions include such issues as for how many years the project is expected to generate emission reductions, the 'payback time' of various technologies (for example, it has been estimated that a 60kW photovoltaic array must produce electricity for 3.7 years before it is carbon neutral) (Murray and Petersen, 2004), and the amount of GHGs destroyed, displaced or stored.

Credit verification occurs when third party verifiers confirm that emission reductions have occurred. A wide variety of accounting methods are used to establish carbon credits in the voluntary markets; some are self-developed by project managers, while others are developed by a third party verifier. Regardless of the system chosen, a few major considerations guide almost all considerations of credit quality (Hamilton, 2006):

- *Additionality:* The project must create reductions over and beyond a business-as-usual scenario, and there must be some assurance that the project would not occur without the funding provided by carbon credits. (For more on additionality, see Box 2.1.)
- *Permanence:* The project must be able to guarantee GHG mitigation over the stated time period. This is especially important in long-term projects, such as ex ante (pre-pay) reforestation in which risks such as a fire would affect the delivery of credits. Indeed, all types of sequestration projects need to ensure that the carbon stored either in trees or underground will not some day be released into the atmosphere.
- *Leakage:* The project must not transfer emissions to another location outside the project area. Leakage occurs when emission reductions at one site or point of time indirectly drive increased emissions from another activity outside of the project boundary. For example, if a forestry project limits logging in one

area, developers should consider the possibility that the source of deforestation will move and simply occur elsewhere.

- *Double counting:* The project must avoid double counting its emissions reductions. Double counting can occur when more than one organization takes credit for owning or retiring offsets. Accurate and publicly available inventories and registries can help resolve this problem. For example, direct and indirect emissions should be inventoried and reported separately.
- *Ex ante and ex post accounting:* In *ex ante* accounting, credits are sold before they are produced; in *ex post* accounting they are sold after. The former entails more risk, commands lower prices and requires stringent guarantees (not to mention ongoing monitoring).
- *Co-benefits:* While the primary goal of carbon credits is to offset GHGs, many types of projects provide additional benefits, such as reductions of other pollutants, contributions to local communities, or habitat for biodiversity. Co-benefits range dramatically between project types, but are an important factor for many individuals and institutions purchasing emission reductions voluntarily. Co-benefits may also represent additional revenue streams for investors. Electricity sales, sales of other pollution credits, or timber sales represent financial co-benefits. It is important, however, that customers understand which co-benefits have been parcelled off and which will remain 'bundled' with the carbon offset. It is also important to understand who gets a project's co-benefits.

When a project's emission reductions have been verified in accordance with a particular certification standard and endorsed by the organization issuing the certification, it is common to say that the resulting carbon credits have been certified. In the Kyoto market, CERs refer to carbon credits that have been approved by the CDM Executive Board. Certification in the voluntary markets is a more general term suggesting that an institution with a recognized set of requirements has endorsed the credits in question with a stamp of approval. Most project developers finance the verification of their carbon emissions reductions before selling them to either intermediaries or end consumers in the voluntary markets. In general, buyers have increasingly asked for certified credits as one means of ensuring that they receive credits from projects that are real, additional and verifiable. They have therefore often preferred third party verification to in-house verification. Suppliers have also embraced the idea of standards as a means of proving their legitimacy. Third party verification is a requirement of the CDM and for most standards, but it is not required in the 'over-the-counter' (OTC) market and is not always utilized (though its utilization is increasing).

In response to the high transaction costs and confusion caused by the wide range of offerings in the voluntary markets, more than a dozen organizations have developed standards or certification programmes. Certification can be an extremely beneficial tool to ensure a consistent level of quality, reduce transaction costs for buyers and build consumer trust. As a tool of legitimacy and fungibility in the marketplace, third party verification and standards could be considered priceless. However, they are not without financial cost. For example, in 2007 the cost of verifying a project to the Community, Climate and Biodiversity (CCB) Standards ranged from $5400 to $15,400. Likewise, the cost of having a credit validated and issued by the VER+ Standard ranged from $7700 to $23,100 in 2007 (Kollmuss et al, 2008). Hence, while it appears that credits verified to a third party standard may sometimes earn a premium over non-verified credits, buyers are paying not only for value, but also for the associated costs. In some cases, especially for smaller projects in developing countries, these costs may still create CDM-like hurdles for developers and simply take too much funding away from the goal of the project: GHG emission reductions.

To date, discord surrounding the large number and variety of certification programmes in the market has caused some confusion among buyers. To address this, several organizations – including the World Wildlife Fund and Ecosystem Marketplace – have developed publicly available reports for buyers to compare standards. Table 2.2 lists some of the standards and certification programmes available for voluntary carbon credits. For more information on any of the standards listed below, see Appendix 2.

Table 2.2   *Major certification programmes/standards available or soon to be available for the voluntary carbon offset markets as of mid-2008*

CCAR Climate Action Reserve	A set of protocols for forestry, agriculture, and landfill gas projects, as well as a registry for credits from projects verified to CCAR protocols.
CarbonFix	Certifies only forestry projects and offers a platform for purchasing credits on its website.
CCB Standards	A set of project design standards for land-based carbon management projects that simultaneously generate climate, biodiversity and sustainable development benefits.
CCX	An internal standard for the listing of credits (including those from offset projects) on its exchange, including the requirement that credits be verified by a CCX-approved third party verifier.
Gold Standard for VERs	A third party standard for carbon credits generated by renewable energy and energy efficiency projects with sustainable development benefits. Version 2.0 was released in October 2008.
Green-e Climate	A certification system for retail offset providers retiring carbon credits for final buyers.
Greenhouse Friendly	An Australian government programme that works with independent verifiers to certify both Australia-based offset projects and carbon neutral products/services.

Table 2.2   *Contd.*

ISO 14064	A GHG accounting, reporting, and verification standard that is part of the international ISO 14000 family of standards. Like the WRI/ WBCSD Protocols, ISO is focused on both corporate and project accounting.
Plan Vivo	A standard designed exclusively for community-based agroforestry projects. It aims to ensure that its projects deliver a host of social, biodiversity, ethical, additional and partnership co-benefits.
Social Carbon	A project design standard based on a sustainable livelihoods approach that focuses on the welfare and potential of local communities as well as their natural resources. It has been used to verify forestry, hydrology and fuel switching projects in Latin America and Portugal.
VER+	A third party standard for offsets based on CDM and JI verification methodologies.
Voluntary Carbon Standard	A third party standard for 'ex post' offsets with its own brand for VCS certified offsets (called Voluntary Carbon Units, or VCUs). VCS 2007 is the most recent version of the standard.
WBCSD/ WRI GHG Protocol for Project & Corporate Accounting	A protocol for carbon accounting incorporated into numerous standards, such as CCAR and ISO 14064 Standards. It is not a certification system or verification standard in itself.

Stage 3: Product distribution

Retailers and carbon fund managers generally select and maintain investments in a portfolio of projects that generate credits over time. Like wine, credits have vintage years denoting the year in which the emission reductions were generated. For example a project that started in 2005 and will last for three years may be able to sell credits for 2005, 2006 and 2007 vintages, or in bulk for the lifespan of the project (such as purchasing a tree that would offset emissions over its 70-year lifespan). Credits sold in 2005 for emission reductions slated to occur in 2006 and 2007 would be *ex ante* credits, and those sold in 2007 for emission reductions in 2006 or 2005 would be *ex post* credits.

Once credits have been verified and/or certified, middlemen often step in either as buyers interested in purchasing credits for on-sale, or as facilitators interested in arranging transactions between buyers and sellers on a fee-for-service basis (the latter are generally referred to as 'brokers').

Retailers

Retailers sell offsets directly to institutional or individual buyers, usually in small amounts and via the internet, from a portfolio of emission reductions that they own. Many online retailers provide carbon footprint calculators on their websites so that users can determine the quantity of emissions to offset, but entering the same inputs into different calculators often generates different results – another example of a situation where 'buyers need beware'.

Pinning down the exact number of offset retailers in the world is a challenge, as not all offset projects are tracked on registries, and information on retailers remains disaggregated. Ecosystem Marketplace has confirmed at least 200 suppliers of voluntary credits (Hamilton et al, 2008). Furthermore, some retailers supply carbon credits in both the regulatory and voluntary markets. Most retailers work on a 'pay-as-you-go' cycle in which they maintain a small inventory of credits and 'top up' when new clients provide funding.

Box 2.1 The additionality debate

In order to create offsets, the emission reductions associated with a project must be additional to those that might be expected under a business-as-usual model. This is important because a real emission of GHG is being 'allowed' into the atmosphere for each offset retired. If the offsets are not additional – if they would have happened anyway – then the net effect on the atmosphere when they are used to neutralize other emissions is negative.

While the concept of additionality is simple, implementing it is not. Debates around additionality have been considered pivotal to the integrity of various sources of carbon credits and the market as a whole (Trexler et al, 2006). While most stakeholders agree that the goal of the market is to reduce total GHGs in the atmosphere, the different perspectives on how this is best accomplished are most acutely illustrated in the additionality and quality debates.

An important concept for most additionality requirements is what is considered to be the baseline: the 'hypothetical description of what would have most likely occurred in the absence of any considerations about climate change mitigation' (WBCSD/WRI, 2008). In order to establish that a GHG offset project has reduced emissions beyond those expected in the baseline, a variety of tests for additionality are used. Five additionality tests are outlined by the World Resources Institute (WRI) / World Business Council for Sustainable Development (WBCSD) Greenhouse Gas Protocol for Project Accounting, a widely accepted standard for project accounting:

- *Investment:* To pass this test, also known as 'financial additionality', developers must prove that potential revenue from the sale of carbon credits is a decisive reason for implementing a project that otherwise would not have occurred. The CDM additionality requirements are based on this concept.

- *Technology*: In order to pass the technology test for additionality, developers must show that the primary benefit derived from the technology used was the reduction of GHG emissions.
- *Regulatory*: The test for regulatory additionality requires that a project reduce emissions below the level required by law.
- Common practice: Similarly, developers must prove that the project reduces GHG emissions more than similar projects employing 'common practice'.
- *Timing*: Some standards require developers to demonstrate that they initiated their project after a specific date. The idea is that the timing of a project can help determine whether or not it was undertaken with the expectation of carbon financing.

Stakeholders regularly debate which tests to use as proof of additionality in the voluntary market. As the WRI/WBCSD Protocol states, 'setting the stringency of additionality rules involves a balancing act' (www.ghgprotocol.org/). For example, additionality criteria that are too lenient may undermine the effectiveness of a GHG reduction programme. Conversely, overly stringent criteria could place burdensome limitations on creating valid GHG emissions, excluding otherwise worthy project activities and delaying project development.

Since there is no 'technically correct' answer to the question of additionality, opinions on the ideal stringency of additionality in the voluntary market range dramatically. Some practitioners argue that additionality was not a critical factor at that stage in the development of carbon markets and that the key goal should be to create financial incentives for reducing GHGs. Some have added that the additionality argument is actually counter-productive and that excessive concerns about additionality are reducing the effectiveness of the market by increasing gridlock on the path to establishing effective trading frameworks. Many have argued that a major benefit of the voluntary markets is that they provide an arena where projects can receive funding without passing strict additionality requirements. For example, Toby Janson-Smith, Director of Conservation International's Ecosystem Services investment programme, argues that standard additionality tests exclude some of the best projects from an environmental and sustainable development perspective – namely, projects that are good for the climate, good for biodiversity and good for local communities (Janson-Smith, 2006).

Others feel that specific additionality tests are an essential piece of developing credibility in the market, arguing that strict adherence to high standards is especially important to ensure offset buyers that the money they've used to purchase offsets will make a difference on the ground. Without such additionality requirements, market analysts, such as Mark Trexler of EcoSecurities, note that because the voluntary markets are so small, their demand could be met by 'false positive' or non-additional offsets, leaving little incentive for investing in truly additional offsets. If consumers can't tell the difference between offsets, they'll purchase the less expensive choice, 'But you can't get real, additional GHG offsets for $1/ton' (Trexler, 2006).

While a retailer's project portfolio may change over time, its transparency to consumers – together with the stringency and standards it uses when selecting projects – is what allows for product differentiation. Project portfolios usually include both emission reductions projects and sequestration projects, but it is worth noting that many retailers choose to work only with emission reductions projects or only with sequestration projects. For a list of voluntary offset retailers, see Appendix 4.

Aggregators and wholesalers

Aggregators and wholesalers sell offsets in bulk and often have ownership of a portfolio of credits. An aggregator serves as an administrative and trading representative for a number of small offset projects, typically on an exchange. By 'pooling' the offsets generated by multiple projects, aggregators reduce the participation cost for project owners, for whom the costs of entering the marketplace as a stand-alone project would have been prohibitive. On the Chicago Climate Exchange (CCX), aggregators oversee the verification of the projects they work with, trade on behalf of project owners and make sure projects comply with CCX requirements. Wholesalers buy emission reductions from project developers and sell them in large quantities to final (usually large institutional) buyers.

Brokers

Brokers work to facilitate transactions between institutions and offset project developers but do not take ownership of credits. Just as they connect buyers and sellers of CERs purchased under the CDM in the Kyoto compliance markets, brokers also provide trading services for VERs in the voluntary markets. Whereas exchanges are preferred for large transaction volumes, frequent trades and standardized products or contracts, brokers are typically used for trading non-standardized products or contracts, often in smaller volumes (Kollmuss et al, 2008). Brokers currently working in the voluntary markets include Evolution Markets, M F Global Limited and CantorCO2e, and others.

Exchanges

Currently, the largest exchange in the world trading voluntary carbon credits is the CCX, and access to the exchange is restricted to members. Though joining the CCX is voluntary, members agree to be bound by its emissions cap and schedule for reductions. The exchange briefly had links to the regulated markets in 2006, when at least 1000 European Union Allowances (EUAs) –'rights to emit' under the EU Emissions Trading Scheme (EU ETS) – were transferred into the CCX by a multinational member. However, by the end of 2006, EUA prices for 2007 contracts plummeted, and this link between the two markets was suspended in 2007.

Recently a handful of other exchanges, including the Asia Carbon Exchange, the Green Exchange, and Climex have either opened themselves up to VER trades generally or announced that they would soon do so, though as of late 2008, the number of credits traded via these other exchanges was limited.

Registries

Carbon credit registries provide a host of services to the carbon markets. They're designed to track credit transactions and ownership, reduce the risk that a single credit can be sold to more than one buyer (which is one form of double counting), and increase transparency in the marketplace. Because they serve all of these roles, registries have come to be seen as a fundamental tool allowing for market efficiency and legitimacy.

Registries can be grouped into two categories: emissions inventories and carbon credit accounting systems. Emissions inventories track organizations' GHG emissions and reductions, primarily pre-regulation or early action emission reductions, and help entities set baselines. Joel Levin of the California Climate Action Registry (CCAR), a California state-created emissions inventory that also serves as a credit accounting system, notes that this type of registry is 'measuring the beans, not tracking the trades'. In addition to CCAR, emissions inventories include the US Department of Energy 1605(b) Program for voluntary GHG reporting, the Canadian GHG Challenge Registry, the World Economic Forum Global Greenhouse Gas Registry, and The Climate Registry (in the US).

For their part, carbon credit accounting registries are designed specifically to track the trades. Mitchell Feierstein of Cheyne Capital Management Ltd describes the carbon markets as creating 'a substantial new commoditized, fungible asset class'. To keep tabs on this asset class, credit accounting registries track only verified emission reductions after they have become carbon credits, often utilize serial numbers as an accounting tool, and generally incorporate screening requirements such as third party verification to a specific offset standard. Accounting registries include the Bank of New York's Global Registry and Custody Service, the verifier TÜV SÜD's BlueRegistry, APX, TZ1 and several registries connected with offset standards.

Other carbon credit accounting registries are designed to underscore an exchange, such as the CCX Offset Registry and the Asia Carbon Registry. In addition, some retailers – such as the Carbon Neutral Company and MyClimate – and third party standard organizations – such as the Gold Standard and Voluntary Carbon Standard – have also created their own registries to track credits they've sold or verified. Some registries even track both emission reductions and carbon credit sales, such as Environmental Resources Trust's (ERT) American Carbon Registry (formerly known as the GHG Registry) and CCAR.

Stage 4: Product 'consumption'

Consumers in the voluntary carbon markets may make a one-time purchase, or they may choose to work with an intermediary in an ongoing relationship, receiving credits from a project or a portfolio of projects year after year. Additionally, they can purchase a credit with the intention to hold onto it forever ('retiring' the credit) or resell the credit at a later date (and thus transferring ownership of the reduction to someone else). In general, carbon credits are consumed in order to offset one of four types of emissions:

Institutional emissions: Companies, non-profit organizations and government agencies may purchase carbon credits in order to offset the emissions generated by their facilities and employees in the course of doing business, such as emissions from commuting, energy use, manufacturing, etc. These emissions are often referred to as direct or internal emissions. In 2007, two-thirds of entities purchasing voluntary offsets did so to offset their total or a portion of their institutional emissions (Hamilton et al, 2008). In some cases organizations offset a range of emissions, such as from employee commuting, airline travel, products produced and electricity. In other cases, companies only offset one source of these emissions, such as airline travel or electricity.

Example. HSBC purchased carbon offsets in order to neutralize its group-wide emissions for the last quarter of 2005. To offset the total emissions amount (170,000 tons of carbon dioxide), HSBC bought 170,000 tons of carbon offset credits from four offset projects around the world: the Te Apiti wind farm in North Island, New Zealand; an organic waste composting project in Victoria, Australia; the Sandbeiendorf agricultural methane capture project in Sandbeiendorf, Gemany; and the Vensa Biotek biomass co-generation project in Andhra Pradesh, India. 'A large-scale collective effort is going to be needed to address climate change. Governments must play their part, and help the public to make informed decisions,' said Francis Sullivan, HSBC's adviser on the environment. 'Banks should also do their bit.' (HSBC, 2005; The Climate Group, 2005)

Product life cycle emissions: Companies, to date, have been less willing to offset the emissions generated by the use of their products (known as their indirect or external emissions) as they have been the emissions associated with their manufacture. While market observers expect this may change in the coming years as companies buy credits in order to develop carbon neutral products for their customers (Rau, 2006), the share of offsets purchased for product life cycle emissions remains small, at 3 per cent of total volume transacted in both 2006 and 2007. Carbon neutral products generally carry a price premium and are marketed as carbon neutral in much the same way that organically produced food products are marketed as environmentally sound. Theoretically, companies could purchase offsets in order to offset their external emissions as a matter of corporate social responsibility without using them towards the certification of carbon neutral products, but this is less likely since most companies will capitalize on a marketing opportunity when and where possible.

Example. BP launched a carbon neutral fuel product in Australia. As part of its Global Choice programme, BP offers its commercial customers the opportunity to offset some of their GHG emissions, either by paying more for an ultimate grade gasoline that comes with a company promise to offset the emissions generated by its use, or by partnering to purchase offsets outright. As of 2008, BP has neutralized more than

2 million metric tons of emissions through its Global Choice programme, equivalent to taking 400,000 cars off the road. 'We do it because we fundamentally believe that we need to tackle climate change, whether it be from our own operations or customers using our products,' said Kerryn Schrank, business adviser for future fuels at BP. 'Offsets are going to be important for the transport sector for the next 20 years or so, until we can get cleaner transport options' (Biello, 2005).

Event emissions: In recent years, steering committees for high-profile events have elected to take events carbon neutral through the purchase of large numbers of carbon credits. As credits become more readily available and certification programmes gain more trust in the coming years, offsetting event emissions may become common practice for many political, athletic and social events. Entire event planning companies have emerged to capitalize on interest in 'green' events.

Example. FIFA offset the 2006 World Cup through a voluntary 100,000-ton carbon offset programme, called the Green Goal Initiative. Although official figures are a closely guarded secret, the budget for carbon neutrality is estimated at 1 million euros, which comes to an average price of ten euros per ton of carbon offset (Zwick, 2006; www.myclimate.org).

Individual emissions: While individuals' emissions can include travel and electricity emissions (described above), it deserves its own category because of its significance to the movement against climate change. Many social sector organizations consider it the most important type of transaction because it allows individuals to take action against climate change, thus increasing public awareness of the market, and enabling civic action where public policy has not yet imposed regulation. Individual consumers purchase carbon credits in order to offset any portion or all of their daily activities. Interestingly, while sales to individuals represented only 5 per cent of the voluntary markets in 2007 (by transaction volume), they accounted for a greater volume than sales to government entities, which totalled only 0.4 per cent of the market in 2007!

Example. Cyd Gorman calculates the emissions from her commute to and from work using a carbon calculator and then pays TerraPass – a business that buys carbon credits and renewable energy certificates on the voluntary market and then sells them on to individual consumers – to offset them for her. 'Think of it as Kyoto for commuters,' says Dan Neil of the Los Angeles Times (Neil, 2005).

How does the market work?

While the simplified supply chain just discussed is useful in understanding how carbon credits generally get to market, it should be noted that it is difficult to depict the market properly using a linear supply chain because a single participant can occupy more than one role. Instead, the model below gives a more realistic sense of how the voluntary carbon markets currently function.

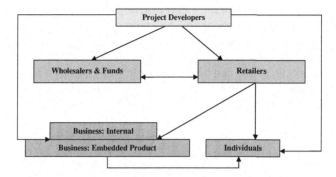

Figure 2.2 *A model of common types of transactions in the voluntary carbon markets*

While organizations that offset events, activities or products tend to purchase offsets from retailers, large corporations with commitments to carbon neutrality generally skip this step and work directly with project developers or brokers, who connect them with project developers. Major examples include BP Global Choice and Cinergy, which originally sourced projects (through the Commonwealth Bank and a tender process, respectively) and now maintain direct relationships (New Forests, 2005). Meridian Energy sells credits from its Te Apiti wind farm in New Zealand to business and retailers through brokers (New Forests, 2005). Theoretically, brokers may connect all kinds of buyers and sellers at any point in the supply chain. In reality, brokers very rarely work with individual consumers, who almost exclusively purchase offsets from retailers or from project developers selling their own credits.

As previously discussed, a select number of businesses also offer embedded carbon neutral products to end-users. Businesses can brand products as carbon neutral, either maintaining their own branding or using a certifier's branding, both of which can help assure customers that the products' life cycle emissions have been offset. For example, the Carbon Neutral Company certifies the carbon neutral claims of companies, products and services and provides its own logo as branding.

Price trends

Since many of the transactions in the voluntary carbon markets occur OTC, and many buyers and sellers guard price information closely, it is difficult to get a perfect read on the wholesale price of carbon credits. Surveying the marketplace we found that prices for the OTC voluntary credits in 2007 covered a wide spread, ranging from \$1.80 to \$300/tCO$_2$e, with the average price being \$6.10/tCO$_2$e (Hamilton et al, 2008). This is almost twice the price of the average CCX credit price (\$3.15/tCO$_2$e) in 2007. This price differential can be explained by the varying sources of demand driving buyers of credits in each market. Much like players participating in a regulated market, CCX members are buying offsets to meet their voluntary cap-and-trade commitments; hence, the average CCX credit price is lower because the co-benefits of a credit are irrelevant. CCX buyers are primarily concerned that the credit meets CCX eligibility criteria and can be used for compliance.

Broadly speaking, prices can be compared at two levels: the cost of the offset project and the market price of the credit sold. Project cost is influenced by three major factors: actual reduction costs (influenced by factors such as project type, size, location, up-front costs vs length of return, profits from co-benefits and additionality); transaction/administration costs; and seller's profit (Butzengeiger, 2005).

Market price is also influenced by several factors. For example, involving intermediaries and additional steps between the project and the buyer, such as brokers, retail sellers, verification, certification and marketing, each increase the price. Similarly, like many commodities, price often varies according to the scale of the purchase. Prices will continue to evolve in the voluntary markets with changes in supply and demand, due not in any small part to expected and existing regulation. For example, US regulation could increase the price of carbon credits across the world.

Importantly, since the attributes contributing to credit quality are only one of the factors influencing price, 'better' credits and higher prices do not always correlate. That said, 'non-additional' credits (which have little environmental value) generally cost less than other types of credits since only the transaction costs involved with claiming the credit contribute to its expense.

What's driving the market?

Heretofore, we have made oblique reference to market drivers (the risk of future regulation, a desire for product differentiation, philanthropic aims, etc.). Now that we have a sense of how supply works in the voluntary carbon markets, it is worth shining a more direct spotlight on the demand for voluntary carbon credits. Is it real? Is it robust? Is it sustainable?

Briefly, one might answer these questions in turn with a yes, a no and a maybe. The best way to assess these questions, however, is to look more carefully at who is buying carbon credits and why. As our earlier discussion of the supply chain revealed, there are two basic types of buyers in the voluntary carbon market: consumers and middlemen. Put simply, consumers buy credits in order to use them to offset the emissions associated with an action, event or product. Middlemen, on the other hand, purchase credits and then sell them on to consumers without making any offset claims of their own.

Both for-profit and not-for-profit institutions act as intermediaries. At the coarsest level, it is fair to say that for-profit middlemen acting as wholesalers or retailers of carbon credits are driven by profit motivations, while their not-for-profit counterparts are generally driven by environmental and sustainable development aims. It should be noted, however, that many of the for-profit organizations operating within this sphere also have philanthropic aims, but believe that a private sector model provides the most sustainable vehicle for driving change.

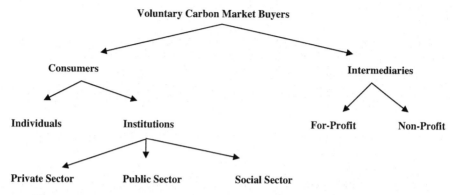

Figure 2.3 *A quick sketch of the different kinds of buyers in the voluntary carbon markets*

Within the consumers category, one can further separate buyers into institutions and individuals. And within the institutions category, it is possible to distinguish between buyers from the private, public and social sector organizations.

Since it is the purchasing behaviour of end consumers that ultimately drives the market, we will look at the motivations that individual and institutional consumers have for buying carbon credits on the voluntary carbon markets (i.e. the buyers listed on the left side of the diagram in Figure 2.3 above).

Individual consumers

In September 2007, the BBC World Service released the results of a poll it commissioned GlobeScan and the Program on International Policy Attitudes (PIPA) to conduct on attitudes towards climate change. The poll covered 22,000 citizens across 21 countries between May and July 2007. In all but one country, more than two-thirds of those polled believed that 'human activity, including industry and transportation, is a significant cause of climate change'. According to Stephen Kull, Director of PIPA, 'The public in developing as well as developed countries agree that action on climate change is necessary' (Globe Scan/BBC, 2007).

Against this backdrop, it is hardly surprising that research suggests individual consumers of carbon credits on the voluntary carbon markets are driven primarily by the sense that addressing climate change is the right thing to do. Though offset purchases made by individuals made up only 5 per cent of transaction volume on the OTC market in 2007, individuals' purchases actually represent a relatively large number of transactions (Hamilton et al, 2008). This is because the credit size of individual purchases tends to be relatively small. For instance, a person wishing to offset a round-trip flight between London and New York City would purchase offsets worth approximately $3tCO_2e$. For comparison, a large business wishing to offset its organizational emissions for one year could easily purchase hundreds of thousands of emissions in a single transaction.

Private sector institutions

In the absence of regulation, financial lenders and shareholder groups are pushing companies in the US, Canada, Australia and New Zealand to develop strategies for managing their carbon footprints. Similarly, European companies that do not fall within the sectors currently regulated under the EU ETS (regulated sectors currently include the energy and industrial sectors) are feeling increasing pressure to act on climate change. Confirming this phenomenon, Ecosystem Marketplace and New Carbon Finance found that private sector institutions accounted for 79 per cent of the OTC voluntary carbon markets transactions in 2007 (Hamilton et al, 2008).

European shipping company DHL, for instance, now offers European customers the option of carbon neutral shipping service, and hopes to extend the option to customers in the Asia–Pacific region before the end of 2008. (Shipping is currently not included as a regulated sector under the EU ETS.) The service, *GOGREEN*, gives customers the option to offset the emissions of their deliveries for a price premium of 3 per cent over standard shipping charges, which the company uses to invest in fuel vehicle technology, reforestation and solar energy projects. According to Ad Ebus, CEO of DHL Express Europe, 'Environmental responsibility is an integral part of living up to our corporate values and we see an increasing number of our global business customers seeking ways to reduce their environmental impact' (DHL, 2007).

Rob Seely, General Manager of Sustainable Development at Shell Canada, says his company views the voluntary carbon markets as a risk management tool. Specifically, the voluntary carbon markets offer Shell Canada the chance to learn about carbon markets in advance of its participation in any future regulatory market, while also helping the company manage its reputation. 'We are part of the problem,' says Seely, 'we need to be part of the solution' (Seely, 2006).

Amy Davidsen, Director of Environmental Affairs at JPMorgan Chase, cites similar reasons for her institution's interest in the market: 'We really see the voluntary carbon markets as an opportunity' (Davidsen, 2006). Davidsen's assertion that companies are beginning to see action on climate change as an opportunity, not just a risk, is important. While risk may drive a few companies to enter the carbon market, opportunity stands to attract many more. So far, the financial sector and the insurance industry seem to be at the head of the class when it comes to structuring products and services that might allow them to profit from the carbon market. 'Now that carbon increasingly has a value, you can either capture it or face risk,' says Francis Sullivan, HSBC's Adviser on the Environment (Wright, 2006).

As another indicator of growing corporate interest in low carbon and carbon neutral operations, the Carbon Disclosure Project's (CDP) most recent survey of corporate carbon emissions yielded the highest response rate to date. The CDP was launched by a global group of institutional investors to pressure businesses to report on their carbon emissions footprint and what they were doing to manage it. The project sends out a survey to the world's largest companies and then publishes the results on its website. Seventy-seven per cent (383 companies) of the Fortune 500 companies polled in the 2007 survey provided emissions data about their operations, an increase in response rate of almost 1000 per cent compared with the first year the survey was conducted in 2003, when only 35 companies responded (45 per cent of those polled in 2003).

Responding to the boom in corporate interest in reducing their carbon footprints, Nick Robbins, Head of Socially Responsible Investment (SRI) funds at Henderson Global Investors, said, 'At the stage we are now, carbon neutrality can be considered best practice in the financial sector. Such commitments are important for building climate change literacy in the business world' (Wright, 2006). In 2006, Henderson, hoping to understand the distribution of carbon risk across companies, commissioned Trucost to profile the carbon emissions of the top 100 listed companies in the UK, the FTSE 100. 'For us, the results of the Carbon 100 pointed to three critical questions for the future,' he says. 'Who owns carbon, who insures carbon, and increasingly, who banks carbon. With the decline in pollution-intensive manufacturing in Western Europe and North America, public pressure on banks that finance such industries in developing countries is likely to rise' (Wright, 2006).

Insurance companies, for their part, are developing new tools and fine-tuning already existing products to help commercial clients prepare for future climate-related risks. Reinsurance giant Swiss Re developed the world's first insurance product for CDM transaction risk for RNK Capital, insuring against the uncertainty of project registration under the Kyoto Protocol. According to Ben Lashkari, head of emissions at Swiss Re's Environmental and Commodity Markets, 'The policy provides liquidity, it provides confidence, and it basically makes the carbon market more of a mature, functioning market' (Hall, 2006).

While still mostly directed at the compliance carbon markets, insurance products like those pioneered by Swiss Re may be a harbinger of insurance products in the pipeline for the voluntary carbon markets. These new and refined products include coverage for companies using new technologies that have not been recently tested, and coverage for companies having to offset energy use by purchasing carbon credits. American International Group, Inc (AIG) recently developed a product aimed at ethanol producers, specifically providing insurance to lenders in case of a delay in production due to the use of largely untested technology. 'We developed a product that would insure for those risks, where the policy proceeds could be used for one of two things,' said Ranjini Pillay, Vice President of underwriting at AIG. 'One is if there is underperformance in the acceptance test, you have additional monies to bring it up to acceptance, and the second one being to potentially pay the banks while you are tweaking the system' (Zuill, 2008).

In general, private companies participate in the voluntary markets for the following reasons:

- *Corporate responsibility*: Believing in a societal obligation to take action against climate change.
- *Public relations/branding*: Wanting to improve public image to appease shareholders, gain customers/investors, and/or attract employees (through 'good actor' perception).

- *Investment*: Purchasing offsets with the intention to resell them for a higher price in the future.
- *Pre-compliance buys*: Purchasing offsets in anticipation of future regulation.
- *Climate-influenced business model*: Buying offsets out of a belief that climate change may or will affect the success of the company.
- *Product sales*: Wanting to gain the competitive edge over similar products in the marketplace, appease customers who are increasingly seeking carbon neutral products, or generate a price premium in the market.

For its report *Forging a Frontier: State of the Voluntary Carbon Markets 2008*, Ecosystem Marketplace, in partnership with New Carbon Finance, surveyed 150 offset suppliers about the motivations of their buyers. Suppliers cited corporate responsibility as the most common reason for buying offsets, with PR/branding benefits the second most common. Investment was cited as the least important motivation, followed by climate-influenced business model and anticipation of regulation (Hamilton et al, 2008).

Public sector institutions

Governments at the local, regional and federal level have all emerged as voluntary buyers of carbon credits, though their share of OTC market transactions remains very low (0.4 per cent in 2007). As of mid-2008, 30 US cities had signed up to calculate and report their carbon footprints to the Carbon Disclosure Projects, and eight cities were registered as full members of the CCX (Aspen, Berkeley, Boulder, Chicago, Fargo, Oakland, Portland, and Melbourne, Australia). Three US counties are also registered as full members of the CCX. And the UK government recently announced it would buy carbon credits in order to take all of its operations carbon neutral.

The race to be the first to become carbon neutral appears to have taken hold at multiple levels of government. Entire countries are vying to become the first nation to claim carbon neutrality, with the current contestants being Costa Rica, New Zealand, Iceland, Norway and Vatican City. (For the record, Vatican City claims to have already reached carbon neutral status through tree planting in Hungary, but critics have noted that true carbon neutrality should be achieved at home.) The United Arab Emirates is even building what it hopes will be the world's first, self-contained 'zero carbon' city – in the desert of Abu Dhabi.

What's driving these decisions? Public sector institutions probably have two primary reasons for entering the voluntary carbon markets as buyers. For one, they are interested in advancing the markets as a means of attracting private sector capital towards costly environmental problems. Second, they sense their constituencies' desire for action on climate change and so want to be seen as leading by example.

Social sector institutions

Here we define social sector organizations as non-governmental or not-for-profit institutional buyers. This type of buyer is driven by three primary motivations: the importance of 'walking the talk', philanthropic aims that range from ecological restoration to sustainable development, and public relations benefits. For non-profits in the environmental and other fields, having a climate-influenced business model also serves as a major motivation for buying offsets.

While many environmental organizations remain sceptical of the voluntary carbon markets – citing concerns ranging from fears that carbon offsets are replacing self-generated reductions, to concern about the legitimacy of offsets – many environmental organizations do believe that markets provide a promising new approach to conservation finance. Among them are some of the world's largest environmental organizations, including The Nature Conservancy (which sells carbon offsets generated by its own conservation projects), World Wildlife Fund and Environmental Defense Fund, as well as many smaller environmental organizations. It is important to note here that each of these institutions, like most environmental groups, supports offsets of high quality and with the understanding that offsets, alone, will not solve the problem of climate change.

There are also a number of corporate foundations, universities and political organizations – both national and international – that have taken it upon themselves to seed the voluntary carbon markets by stepping in as buyers of carbon credits. The key driver of demand among these buyers, then, is the degree to which they believe the market can drive environmental and social benefits.

Evolving financial instruments

As market size, climate legislation and interest in carbon neutrality have increased, so has institutional investment in the voluntary carbon markets. ICF International reported 54 carbon funds, the majority focused on the regulated market, managing 12 billion euros in 2007 (Zwick, 2007). Though the definition of carbon fund varies, in ICF's case it refers to 'a vehicle that collects money from different investors and then disburses this money to buy carbon credits or to invest equity or provide loans to emission reductions projects in order to provide returns either in carbon credits or in cash to the investor' (Zwick, 2007).

While they're not nearly as present as they are in the regulated markets, carbon funds focused specifically on voluntary carbon offsets have begun to emerge. Cheyne Capital Management Limited started the Cheyne Carbon Fund (formerly known as the Cheyne Climate Wedge Fund), the world's first voluntary carbon offset fund, in July 2005. The fund identifies, purchases and manages carbon offsets for large-scale corporate and institutional buyers. 'Recognizing the substantial demand and need for the creation of a credible commoditized asset class in fungible voluntary carbon credits in 2005 provided by creditworthy counterparties,' remarked Mitchell Feierstein, Senior Portfolio Adviser to the fund, 'we developed a high quality standardized offset product for use by our numerous Fortune 500 clients.'

Additionally, more carbon funds initially focused on compliance credits are adding voluntary offset credits to their portfolios. European Carbon Fund, launched in 2005, for instance, includes voluntary carbon offsets as a small percentage of its portfolio. The World Bank has also established carbon funds that provide financing for projects intending to sell into the voluntary markets, in addition to funding CDM projects.

Market trends

While tracking the voluntary market, we've seen continued growth in both the OTC and CCX sides of the voluntary markets. It appears that drivers in the of the voluntary carbon markets are set to grow in the coming years, but it should be remembered that the market is far from mainstream at this point and uncertainty abounds. Fortunately, registries, standards and exchanges are evolving to help streamline the voluntary carbon markets and consolidate market information as potential buyers push for increased transparency. It should become easier, then, for buyers and sellers to grasp both the risks and the opportunities associated with this dynamic market in the coming years.

References

Arnold, T. Interviewed by Amanda Hawn, July 2006

Bank of New York Company (2006) 'The Bank of New York creates global registrar and custody service for voluntary carbon units', *Business Wire*, 19 June

Biello, D. (2005) 'Climate friendly fuels', The Ecosystem Marketplace, www.ecosystem marketplace.com

Butzengeiger, S. (2005) 'Voluntary compensation of GHG emissions: Selection criteria and implications for the international climate policy system', Report No 1 by The HWWI Research Programme International Climate Policy, Hamburg Institute of International Economics, Hamburg

Davidsen, A. (2006) Presentation at GreenT Forum: Raising the Bar for Voluntary Environmental Credit Markets, New York, 1–2 May

DHL (2007) 'DHL's GoGreen service helps World Economic Forum meet its carbon neutral promise for Davos', press release, 18 January

Hall, J. (2006) 'Climate change: For insurers, the best defense may be a good offense', The Ecosystem Marketplace, www.ecosystemmarketplace.com

Hamilton, K. (2006) 'Navigating a nebula: Institutional use of the U.S. voluntary carbon market', Masters thesis at the Yale School of Forestry

Hamilton, K., Sjardin, M., Marcello, T. and Xu, G. (2008) 'Forging a frontier: State of the voluntary carbon markets 2008', The Ecosystem Marketplace and New Carbon Finance, May

Hawn, A. (2005) 'eBay shoppers and subsistence farmers meet on virtual ground', The Ecosystem Marketplace, www.ecosystemmarketplace.com

HSBC (2005) 'HSBC carbon neutral pilot project', www.hsbc.com/1/ PA_1_1_S5/content/assets/csr/carbon_neutral_brochure_oct05.pdf

Janson-Smith, T. Interviewed by Kate Hamilton, July 2006

Kollmuss, A., Zink, H. and Polycarp, C. (2008) *Making Sense of the Voluntary Carbon Markets: A Comparison of Carbon Offset Standards*, World Wildlife Fund, Germany

Kvale, L. Interviewed by Walker Wright, July 2006

Murray, M. E. and Petersen, J. E. (2004) 'Payback and currencies of energy, carbon dioxide and money for a 60kW photovoltaic array', Technical Report, Oberlin College, Oberlin, Ohio

Neil, D. (2005) 'TerraPass eases drivers' minds', *Los Angeles Times*, 2 February

New Forests Advisory Pty Ltd (2005) '2005 Global Retail Carbon Market Report', prepared for the Ecosystem Marketplace

Rau, A. Interviewed by Amanda Hawn, June 2006

Seely, R. (2006) Presentation at GreenT Forum: Raising the Bar for Voluntary Environmental Credit Markets, New York, 1–2 May

The Climate Group (2005) 'Carbon down profits up' 2nd edn, *Environmental Finance*

Trexler, M. Interviewed by Kate Hamilton, May 2006

Trexler, M., Broekhoff, D. J. and Kosloff, L. H. (2006) 'A statistically driven approach to offset based GHG additionality determinations: What can we learn', *Sustainable Development Law and Policy*, vol VI, issue 2, American University Washington College of Law, Washington DC

World Business Council for Sustainable Development / World Resources Institute (WBCSD/WRI) (2008) 'GHG protocol for project accounting', www.ghgprotocol.org/files/ghg_project_protocol.pdf

Wright, C. (2006) 'Carbon neutrality draws praise, raises expectations for HSBC', *The Ecosystem Marketplace*, www.ecosystemmarketplace.com

Zuill, L. (2008) 'Insurers broaden coverage for climate change risks', *Reuters*, 18 June, www.reuters.com/article/rbssInsuranceMultiline/idUSN1826863020080618

Zwick, S. (2006) 'Green goal: Soccer enters the carbon markets', The Ecosystem Marketplace, www.ecosystemmarketplace.com

Zwick, S. (2007) 'Carbon funds: In the driver's seat', The Ecosystem Marketplace, www.ecosystemmarketplace.com

3

RECs vs Offsets: The Debate Continues

At a recent US-based conference, voluntary carbon wonks were getting stirred up and the mood was divisive. The issue? The appropriate use of renewable energy certificates (RECs) as offsets in the voluntary carbon markets. On one side of the debate, stakeholders like Ron Luhur from Environmental Defense Fund were adamant that, with rare exceptions, RECs simply cannot be converted into carbon offsets and cross over to the voluntary carbon markets.

'With RECs you're claiming an indirect reduction somewhere else on the grid that may or may not happen, and clarity of ownership of the reduction is uncertain,' Luhur said. He emphasized that ownership of emissions reductions in the case of large-grid renewable energy projects, which source most of the power in the US, is particularly hard to prove.

Likewise, another vocal critic, Michael Gillenwater, a Princeton researcher and the head of the Greenhouse Gas Management Institute, argues that using RECs as offsets creates a host of conceptual problems. All of them can all be traced to the fact that at its core, an REC guarantees clean energy generation, not carbon emission reductions. 'It's sort of like claiming that an emissions allowance isn't just a tracking device, it embodies everything good with that power plant,' says Gillenwater. 'Imagine a [Certified Emissions Reduction] that doesn't just tell you emissions have been reduced, but also how many jobs have been created. You can take it to absurd levels pretty quickly' (Rose, 2008).

Across the table, others like Lars Kvale from APX (formerly with the Center for Resource Solutions) argue that carbon finance should support renewable energy projects in the US much as it does internationally. 'The question is not whether RECs are offsets, but whether building new additional renewable energy generation in the United States reduces GHG emissions? The answer to this is clearly in the affirmative.'

At the same time, suppliers like Village Green and guidance entities like EPA Climate Leaders have suggested compromise scenarios such as allowing RECs to count towards carbon neutral goals when used to match electricity use.

Before we delve into the current state of debate more deeply, let's run through what RECs are and how they are traded.

The US voluntary REC market and how it interacts with the carbon market

Lori A. Bird and Walker L. Wright
National Renewable Energy Laboratory

Recognition of the need to decrease the amount of electricity derived from fossil fuels has increased interest in renewable energy products – which harness wind, sunlight, plant matter or heat from the earth's core – to produce electricity that is environmentally friendly. In turn, this interest has led governments to mandate the incorporation of more renewable power sources into grids around the world. And consumers are increasingly purchasing renewable energy for their own electricity needs.

What are RECs?

RECs represent the renewable attributes of a unit, typically 1 MWh of electricity generated from renewable sources. The renewable attributes of that electricity are then sold separately as an REC; one REC may be issued for each unit of renewable electricity produced. In other words, programmes have been established that separate renewable electricity generation into two commodities:

1   RECs representing the green attributes, or social and environmental benefits, of renewable energy generation.
2   Electricity produced by a renewable generator delivered to the grid, where it blends with electricity from conventional generators in a generic 'soup' of electrons following the path of least resistance (Gewin, 2005).

Like the global carbon market, the US REC market features both compliance and voluntary segments. There is no one distinct market for RECs but rather a potpourri of fragmented markets in which prices and eligible renewable energy resources vary. We will turn first to the compliance side of the market.

REC compliance markets

Many US states have implemented Renewable Portfolio Standards (RPS) to require energy companies and utilities to use renewable energy sources to provide some percentage of the electricity they sell to consumers each year. Typically, utilities may meet RPS requirements in any of three ways: they may build renewable energy sources themselves, they may buy renewable energy from projects connected to the grid or they may purchase RECs from renewable energy generators. While a few states have not allowed the use of RECs for RPS compliance, generally, regulated utilities may employ all three of these strategies, but it is worth noting that RECs – because they generally are not bound to the same geographic

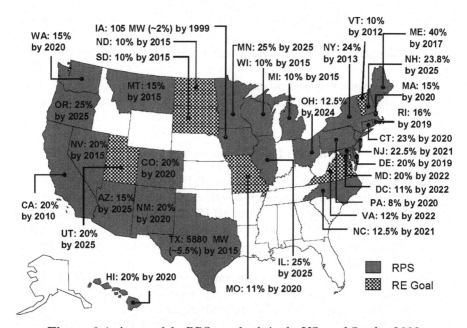

Figure 3.1 *A map of the RPS standards in the US as of October 2008*

Note: In the US, state governments frequently update RPS standards

Sources: National Renewable Energy Laboratory and the Database of State Incentives for Renewable Energy

or physical constraints as commodity electricity – represent the most flexible mechanism for compliance.

Collectively, states with aggressive RPS schemes are creating significant demand for RECs, and this demand will accelerate in future years as renewable energy targets increase and new policies take effect. To date, more than half of US states have renewable portfolio standards in place and in recent years many states have significantly increased their renewable energy targets. For example, Colorado recently expanded its RPS requirement for the state's investor-owned utilities from 10 per cent to 20 per cent of retail electricity sales by 2020. Collectively, these RPS policies called for 16 million MWh of new renewable energy in 2007. They are expected to lead to the development of a cumulative 5000MW of new renewables' capacity by 2010 and 32,000MW by 2015, if full compliance is achieved (Wiser and Barbose, 2008).

The voluntary REC market

As in the carbon market, the voluntary market for RECs is characterized by a variety of businesses offering a wide array of products. The flexibility of voluntary RECs allows the consumer to support renewable energy development through certificate purchases regardless of where they are located geographically, without having to switch to an alternative electricity provider.

Numerous companies now offer certificate-based green power products, and many now allow individuals and businesses to buy RECs online.[1] In general, voluntary RECs are sold to consumers in one of two ways:

1   As a stand-alone product, either regionally or nationally.
2   Bundled with energy derived from any fuel sources to produce green energy products.

Stand-alone (unbundled) REC products

A growing number of marketers sell unbundled RECs to commercial and individual users who are anxious to support the development of renewable energy projects. For the most part stand-alone RECs are marketed to non-residential consumers such as businesses, universities and government agencies. Recently, unbundled RECs have been the fastest growing portion of the voluntary renewable energy market.

Since commercial consumers often want to support local renewable energy projects for branding purposes and reasons of corporate social responsibility, REC retailers often focus on a defined geographic area. For instance, Pennsylvania-based Community Energy Inc (CEI) – bought by IBERDOLA of Spain in May 2006 – marketed RECs from new wind energy projects in the Mid-Atlantic states to end-use customers in these states. The Bonneville Environmental Foundation (BEF), a non-profit organization based in Portland, Oregon, pursues a similar sales model in the Pacific Northwest, where it sells 'Green Tags' – RECs generated by new wind, solar and biomass projects in Oregon, Washington and Wyoming – to businesses, government agencies and other large energy consumers in the area.

Other retailers ignore geographic boundaries when sourcing RECs for sale as a stand-alone product. Taking advantage of the fact that RECs can be sold across state lines, retailers such as Georgia-based Sterling Planet choose to market RECs sourced from renewable energy generators located throughout the nation.

Bundled products

The second main type of transaction in the voluntary market is the sale of green energy products (with RECs embedded in them) to consumers who are willing to pay price premiums associated with the development of renewable energy sources. When RECs are bundled with electricity and sold as green power, clean power or renewable power, it is worth noting that the use of RECs is often invisible to the consumer. Rather, energy retailers act on behalf of the consumer, purchasing RECs wholesale and retiring them in order to substantiate their claims to the provision of green energy. Many bundled REC products are targeted at residential and small commercial consumers who may have difficulty understanding the concept of an REC.

Market trends

Despite the perception that it is small, the voluntary REC market is approximately on a par with the compliance market with respect to size. However, voluntary market REC prices are generally lower. Estimating the value of the voluntary market is more complicated than that of compliance markets, given the variety of products offered, differences in the price of products sold to residential and non-residential consumers, and the variety of resources used to supply the market. The total voluntary market for renewables (bundled and REC products) has been growing at an annual average rate of nearly 50 per cent in recent years, with the REC portion of the market dominating sales (Bird et al, 2008). Table 3.1 shows annual voluntary market sales of RECs and bundled green power for 2003–2007. Estimates for 2007 are total market size of about 18 million MWh, which represents more than 50 per cent annual growth.

For residential and small commercial customers, RECs often sell for US$15/MWh to $25/MWh ($0.015–$0.025 per kWh), but prices can vary and change quickly over short periods of time. RECs sold to large non-residential consumers sometimes sell at considerable volume discounts. REC prices for voluntary markets have risen in the first half of 2008, compared to previous years. According to data from Evolution Markets, an REC broker, wholesale prices for voluntary RECs in the first half of 2008 were in the order of about $5/MWh or higher, with variability among regions and renewable energy technologies, compared to prices as low as about $2/MWh in 2007 (Evolution Markets, 2007, 2008). The price increases have resulted from increases in both compliance and voluntary market demand, as a number of very large purchases have occurred in the marketplace. In addition, many states have adopted new RPS policies or increased their renewable energy targets. Such increases can impact demand for credits in the voluntary market.

Certification

Certification programmes have been developed to ensure that the promised social and environmental benefits are delivered to end-use consumers. The two largest certifiers of RECs for the voluntary market in the US are the Center for Resource Solutions (CRS) and the Environmental Resources Trust (ERT).

The non-profit CRS established the Green-e Energy programme in 1997 to build consumer confidence in green power during the electricity restructuring process of the mid-1990s. The nation's first voluntary verification and certification programme for renewable electricity products, Green-e Energy sets environmental product standards and requires companies to disclose information about their renewable energy products. Green marketers who wish to transact in Green-e Energy certified products pay an annual fee and agree to an annual audit of their marketing claims and transactions. Green-e Energy also requires all of the environmental attributes, including the carbon benefits, to be included in the REC. In return, the marketers benefit from consumer confidence in their products.

Table 3.1 *Estimated annual voluntary REC sales, 2003–2007 (thousands of MWh)*

Market Sector	2003	2004	2005	2006	2007	% Change 2003/2004	% Change 2004/2005	% Change 2005/2006	% Change 2006/2007
Bundled Products	3200	4500	4700	5100	7500	41%	4%	9%	47%
RECs	660	1700	3900	6800	10,600	161%	126%	75%	56%
Retail Total	**3800**	**6200**	**8500**	**11,900**	**18,100**	**62%**	**37%**	**41%**	**53%**

Source: Bird et al (2008)

The Green-e Energy National Standard is the most widely used certification standard in the US, with more than 70 different marketers offering Green-e Energy certified RECs. Sales of these Green-e Energy certified RECs totalled more than 13 million MWh in 2007, an increase of nearly 60 per cent over 2006 levels (CRS, 2006, 2008). Note that this figure includes wholesale RECs which are also later certified at retail; the figures presented in Table 3.1 for the entire market are smaller because they include only retail sales. Adjusting for the RECs and bundled products that are certified twice (at wholesale and retail), Green-e certifies about two-thirds of the entire voluntary green power market as estimated by NREL. In order to earn Green-e Energy certification, all RECs used in Green-e Energy certified REC products have to be from new renewable facilities, defined as coming online after 1 January 1997. Additionally, the renewable energy used cannot come from a facility that has been mandated by a government agency or produced in order to satisfy a government RPS. All Green-e Energy certified products undergo annual audits on power generation and marketing claims.

ERT defines an REC slightly differently than the CRS. ERT holds that RECs are simply a record of the claim of energy generation placed into the grid. ERT will conduct a post-sale audit to verify that RECs have not been sold or 'counted' more than once. ERT's EcoPower[SM] programme both certifies renewable electricity to meet certain environmental standards and works with suppliers to provide the requested renewable electricity mix to corporations and municipalities (ERT, 2006).

Whichever verification methodology and certification label retailers choose to use, most will attest that third-party verification of a project's RECs has become increasingly important in recent years. Furthermore, if the voluntary market for RECs is to continue growing, all agree that transparency and careful project accounting are necessary to maintain consumer confidence in such an intangible product.

RECs and the voluntary carbon markets

As voluntary carbon markets have expanded, one of the most interesting market trends is the increasing convergence of the voluntary markets for RECs and carbon offsets.

Look closely at many of the contracts for RECs within the US voluntary market, and you will find they mention the greenhouse gas (GHG) emissions that will be avoided as a result of the project generating the REC. In these cases, the demand for RECs could be construed as demand for carbon emission reductions. But the demand for RECs may also be driven by other factors, like the demand for a more diversified energy base. Either way, buyers in the US are increasingly looking to both the REC and carbon markets to advance action on the intertwined issues of energy policy and climate change. As these buyers – and the retailers who respond to them – drive the carbon market and REC market towards one another, two important questions arise. First, what is the appropriate role of RECs? And second, what happens to the REC market if a robust regulated carbon market comes onto the scene in the US?

RECs as offsets: The debate

In recent years, there has been significant debate about the role of RECs as carbon offsets. Proponents assert that RECs should be considered suitable carbon offsets because zero-emitting renewable energy sources create real emissions benefits when they operate and displace fossil fuel-based generation. They argue that RECs can be converted to carbon offsets by determining the amount of CO_2 that is displaced when renewable energy facilities operate in lieu of fossil fuel-burning power plants.

Others argue that RECs cannot be used as offsets because they do not result in additional carbon emissions reductions. They propose that because REC revenues are insufficient by themselves to drive the development of new renewable energy projects, any emissions reductions are not above and beyond business as usual. Mark Trexler, Director of EcoSecurities Global Consulting Services, argues 'selling "non-additional" RECs into the carbon offset market undercuts the additionality requirement that is at the heart of carbon offsets, and could devalue the voluntary carbon offset market'. In addition, some argue that renewable energy sources indirectly reduce emissions because CO_2 reductions are achieved when the renewable energy generators displace fossil fuel generation. Thus, they argue that the renewable energy source does not have clear ownership of the direct emissions reductions and therefore that RECs cannot be claimed as offsets of direct emissions of CO_2 from activities such as driving, air travel, and heating.

To address the lack of consumer standards for carbon offsets, the CRS recently launched a new certification standard, Green-e Climate, which is separate from Green-e Energy, covering retail GHG products sourced from renewable energy facilities as well as other GHG reductions certified to other third party standards. As part of developing this new Green-e Climate programme, a new protocol was created to address issues related to additionality, ownership and RECs for renewable energy facilities in the US. This Green-e Climate Protocol addresses additionality by requiring that renewable energy facilities meet a series of additionality tests, including a performance-based test in order to become eligible for selling carbon offsets. The Green-e Climate programme also includes a methodology for calculating the emissions benefits from renewable energy generation that involves considering baseline emissions from the current generation mix in comparison to those expected from new facilities. To date, a number of retail carbon offset projects have been certified under the programme and are selling Green-e Climate offsets in the US as well as to other domestic and international offset projects (CRS, 2008).

At the same time, the US Environmental Protection Agency (EPA) Climate Leaders programme recently released guidance for its partners, which include many Fortune 500 companies, that limits the use of RECs as a GHG emission reduction tool. EPA allows partners to use RECs that pass an additionality screen to adjust the GHG emissions associated with their indirect emissions (i.e. those not under their direct control, such as power purchases) and provides a methodology for calculating the emissions benefits of REC purchases. However, the programme does not allow the use of RECs as carbon offsets for direct GHG emissions because of the question of ownership of the emissions reductions.

The EPA guidance also establishes an important precedent by creating a performance threshold to address the question of additionality of RECs. Under the guidance, additionality is determined based on 'a level of performance that, with respect to emission reductions, technologies or practices, is significantly better than average compared with recently undertaken practices or activities in a relevant geographic area' (EPA, 2008). Projects that meet the performance threshold are considered additional or beyond that which would be expected under a business-as-usual scenario.

Impact of emerging carbon regulation

Just as some carbon market participants fear the expansion of the voluntary REC market could undermine the voluntary carbon market's ability to drive real benefits, some participants in the REC market have similar concerns about carbon markets. They are concerned that the future expansion of carbon markets in the US could impinge upon the ability of the US REC market to contribute to GHG emission reductions. If emission allowances in a regulated cap-and-trade scheme are granted exclusively to existing emitters rather than renewable energy facilities, then any emission reductions resulting from renewable generation that displaces fossil fuel generation will simply allow the fossil fuel plants to retire fewer allowances. And since these extra allowances can then be sold to other fossil fuel plants enabling them to increase their emissions, the renewable generation would not result in net emissions reductions. Although the renewable facilities would be adding more electricity to the grid, they would have failed to reduce emissions on a system-wide scale. 'Under a cap-and-trade system, the only way to reduce air pollution for the associated pollutant is to reduce the number of allowances,' explains Rob Harmon of the Bonneville Environmental Foundation. 'Without the ability to claim air quality improvements, the demand for new renewable energy will likely be substantially reduced.'

The Regional Greenhouse Gas Initiative (RGGI), which became the first cap-and-trade programme to cover a portion of the US when it took effect in the northeast in 2009, has a mechanism for addressing these concerns by allowing voluntary REC markets to provide carbon benefits in the capped market. Most states participating in the RGGI programme have adopted a 'voluntary market set-aside' for renewable energy and RECs sold to voluntary consumers from renewables in the region. Under this mechanism, states will set aside and retire allowances equivalent to the volume of renewable energy and RECs sold to voluntary purchasers in the region, ensuring that a reduction in CO_2 emissions is achieved. It remains to be seen if similar provisions will be adopted in other cap-and-trade programmes emerging in other regions of the US currently.

On balance

While there is still debate about the use of RECs as offsets for direct GHG emissions, there seems to be general consensus regarding their use for addressing indirect CO_2 emissions, such as those associated with electricity purchases. In addition, people on all sides of the debate agree that additionality is the key consideration; the debate lies primarily in how to determine what is additional. Despite the ongoing debate, both REC and offset markets are continuing to grow at a rapid pace and third party certification standards are emerging to help shape the marketplace.

What the experts think

In order to get a better sense of the arguments for and against crossover between the REC and carbon markets in the US, we have asked two experts to take opposite sides of the debate. In the following section, Rob Harmon, Vice President of Renewable Energy Programs at the Bonneville Environmental Foundation, will describe why he thinks the convergence of the two markets is a positive development in light of new approaches to addressing additionality concerns. Mark Trexler, Director of EcoSecurities Global Consulting Services, will then explain the case against trading RECs into the carbon market.

The ABCs of renewable energy, RECs and greenhouse gas offsets

Rob Harmon
Bonneville Environmental Foundation

There is much discussion in this book about how RECs should or should not interact with the GHG market. The overarching question in the RECs vs carbon offsets debate is: when customers buy renewable energy certificates, under what circumstances should those purchases be considered GHG offsets?

It is useful to approach this question by carefully breaking it down into three questions: Does renewable energy reduce GHG emissions? When customers buy RECs as CO_2 reductions, under what circumstances are those purchases meaningful? How can customers use RECs to offset their organizations' CO_2 emissions?

Question 1: Does renewable energy reduce GHG emissions?

There seems to be general agreement on the following:

- Renewable energy projects are being built and put electricity into the grid when they operate.

- This causes fossil fuel energy facilities to operate less or 'back out'.[2]
- When those fossil fuel facilities are backed out, less fossil fuel is burned and CO_2 emissions are reduced.
- Therefore, when renewable energy facilities operate, CO_2 emissions are indeed reduced.[3] This conclusion is supported by the fact that renewable energy projects are used across the globe as carbon offsets projects under the Kyoto treaty.
- In addition, choices are being made across the country regarding which new resources should be developed. At the beginning of 2008, approximately 140 new coal plants were being considered in the US. Many utilities are making a choice between coal and renewables.
- The results of those choices will have huge implications for US GHG emissions for decades to come.
- Therefore, choosing renewable energy today, if it affects the resource choices currently being made, will drive substantial CO_2 emissions reductions in the future.

Question 2: When customers buy RECs as CO_2 reductions, under what circumstances are these purchases meaningful?

- A widely used measure for determining if carbon offset projects are meaningful is abbreviated R-S-V-P-E: Real, Surplus (or 'Additional'), Verifiable, Permanent and Enforceable.
- RECs are the standard unit of measurement for renewable energy across the country. While it is true that all renewable energy projects generate RECs, not all RECs are eligible for use as carbon offsets in the voluntary market. No one in this debate is suggesting that RECs produced from projects built prior to 1997, when the voluntary renewable energy market began, should be used to mitigate today's CO_2 emissions. Under Green-e Climate rules, RECs *from approved projects* are converted to tons of emissions reductions using standard industry conversion factors.
- An examination of how Green-e Climate Standards stack up against the RSVPE standard shows the following:
  a **Real**: Under Green-e Standards, all green power and REC purchases must be from the metered output of renewable energy facilities. One REC is created when 1MWh of renewable energy is actually delivered to the grid. As discussed earlier, that generation also 'backs out' fossil fuel generation resources, offsetting CO_2 emissions, resulting in real reductions of CO_2 emissions.
  b **Surplus:** This seems to be an area where the most controversy exists. It will be addressed at the end of this section.
  c **Verifiable:** Some critics argue that customers who purchase offsets derived from renewable energy projects cannot be certain of the CO_2 emissions benefits these projects create. This is simply not the case. Output from renewable energy projects is metered and RECs are the mechanisms for tracking that generation. All Green-e certified sales go

through a certification process that is professionally audited. In late 2007 and 2008, government-sponsored REC tracking systems began rolling out across the country. These tracking systems brand each REC generated with a unique serial number to ensure that each REC can be counted once and only once and that the owner of each REC can be clearly identified. Therefore the renewable energy generation is verifiable. The CO_2 emissions vary from region to region and from season to season, but both Green-e and the EPA have protocols for calculating the CO_2 emissions reductions associated with RECs based on the location of the facility. Therefore, the associated reductions in CO_2 emissions are also verifiable. Critics, who suggest that buyers of RECs do not know the amount of emissions reductions they are purchasing, are simply misinformed.

d   **Permanent:** Renewable energy and the associated CO_2 reductions happen in real time. When renewable energy facilities operate, fossil fuel resources burn less fossil fuel. Those emissions reductions occur at the time of generation, and they do not 'leak' back into the system later. Therefore, the reductions are permanent.

e   **Enforceable:** Some have argued that because some GHG emission registries have not yet determined how to track the carbon benefits of renewable energy as offsets, those benefits might be double counted. The fact that these registries lack protocols for handling the transfer of RECs and green power means that they still have work to do, but it is not a reason to undermine the carbon value of renewable energy in the marketplace. Concerns about tracking the reductions are absolutely valid, but the debate should focus on improving the registries to meet the highest practicable standards of transparency and the avoidance of double counting.

In the US there is currently no national regulation of CO_2 emissions. Because the government has not asserted a right of ownership or otherwise modified the CO_2 property right, the RECs and any associated emissions reductions therein belong first to the party owning the renewable generating facility that creates the emissions reductions, and then to any party to whom they sell the REC. This is consistent with the international practices adopted by the Clean Development Mechanism under the Kyoto Protocol as well as the majority of standards operating within the voluntary carbon markets.

Regarding enforcement, Green-e is not a government entity, but it does have a well-established Code of Conduct and a thorough set of audit protocols. Any seller of Green-e certified products who violates the Green-e protocols is notified by Green-e and their Green-e accreditation is revoked. Therefore, the renewable energy production and the associated CO_2 emissions reductions are enforceable.

The additionality debate

Definitions of surplus or 'additionality' seem to be a source of confusion, and at times, controversy. There are several elements in the debate.

The first question one must ask is, 'surplus to what?' Under Green-e Standards, no renewable energy or RECs that are created under any mandate (like a Renewable Portfolio Standard) can be sold into the voluntary market. In addition, no renewable energy or RECs that are being claimed by a utility as serving its customers can be sold into the voluntary market. For example, under Green-e rules, a statement from a utility such as 'we're using wind power' prohibits the sale of those RECs into the voluntary market. Those RECs are considered to be 'rate-based', which means that a project has its costs covered by all of a utility's customers (i.e. its rate base), in which case the benefits of the project belong to the same customers. In addition, Green-e considers *all* renewable energy projects built before 1997 (when the voluntary green power market began) to be rate-based and ineligible to be sold into the voluntary market under Green-e rules. Finally, the Green-e Climate standard excludes all facilities built prior to 2005. The result is that the vast majority of the renewable energy being generated in the US is not available to generate RECs for sale into voluntary markets under Green-e rules.

There are a range of additionality tests in the carbon markets. However, they can be boiled down to just two competing theories: the Project-by-Project Financial Test (used primarily in the Kyoto Clean Development Mechanism programme), and the Performance Test, most commonly used for US-based projects.

Project-by-project financial additionality test

Under this proposed test, an outside party would examine the financial arrangements of all new renewable energy projects seeking credit for their CO_2 reductions. If the outside party determined that the projects would not have been built without the REC premium, it would qualify. If the outside party determined that the project would have been built regardless of the REC premium, it would not qualify. Problems with this type of test include:

- Financial arrangements are rarely consistent as the project moves forward. Revenues and liabilities change during the development process. There is no way to know if the numbers the outside party reviews will represent the final numbers.
- It is easy to manipulate numbers to make it appear that projects are in need of financial help. In fact, this test encourages such behaviour (Young, 2008).
- A consultant-based system creates huge uncertainty that will prove slow and burdensome (Carbon Finance, 2008).

Overall, the fundamental problem with the project-by-project financial additionality test is that it is not structured to take advantage of the power of the market. Critics argue that some REC dollars flow to projects that have already been built. To the contrary, this is *precisely* what an efficient marketplace allows. The REC market allows renewable energy developers to finance and build projects with the commercially reasonable *assumption* that when the RECs are produced, there will be a place to sell them. Such assumptions are how markets work – they are why farmers grow crops and companies build widgets. Supply is produced *in anticipation* of the demand generated in functioning markets.

Some argue that because renewable energy developers need 70 or more dollars per MWh to build a project, the dollars they receive per REC (which is often less than $10) do not materially increase the amount of revenue for the project, and thus do not create additional renewable energy development. This argument overlooks a fundamental reality of the energy marketplace.

Renewable energy developers operate in an ultra-competitive market. To build a renewable energy project, the developer must be able to out-compete the fossil generator in the fight for both financing and long-term energy contracts. In short, if a wind facility can sell electricity less expensively than a coal facility, the wind facility will probably be built. What matters in this competition is not the $70 per MWh that both the coal plant and the wind plant need; what matters is that the sale of the REC (which is often approximately equal to the *profit* on the project) provides the *profitability* that allows the wind plant to be financed. Without the profit, the project will not be built. But, renewables don't just need to be profitable to be built; they need to be *more profitable* and less risky than fossil fuel plants.

In reality, it is impossible to create an objective 'financial additionality' test. Even if it were possible, such a test is not a good idea when the major issue of the day is not whether renewable energy is profitable, but whether it is more or less profitable than developing coal-fired facilities. The Bonneville Environment Foundation (BEF) believes that transparent determinations of additionality, the presence of a functioning REC market, and Green-e rules, provide the necessary demonstration of additionality – and that project-by-project financial yardstick tests are excessively burdensome, frequently inaccurate and not transparent.

Performance-based additionality tests

Considering the failings of financial additionality tests, and the economic principles discussed above, BEF has long supported what are referred to as 'performance' tests. These performance tests set up clear rules regarding which projects can sell their carbon emission reduction value to the market, and which cannot.

Both the Green-e Energy and Green-e Climate programmes use such a test. The California Climate Action Registry also uses a performance approach for its offset protocols. Under this approach, the hard work of examining barriers to eligible projects (including the extent to which such projects are already being deployed) is all completed up front by the certifying body, as opposed to running each individual project through a cumbersome financial additionality test. Performance tests typically require three core elements for a project to be eligible:

- The project must use one of the technology types from an approved list. For instance, Green-e Energy allows wind, solar, landfill and other biogas, small low-impact hydropower, and certain biomass types. The California Climate Action Registry allows projects that capture and destroy landfill methane and

livestock methane.
- The project must have been built after a certain cut-off date. For instance, Green-e Climate projects must be built after 2005.
- The project must not have been mandated to be built by law, regulators or courts.

The virtues of this approach are numerous. But most importantly, it eliminates any bureaucratic barrier to market entry by allowing participation of projects which are deemed, based on conservative analysis, to have been incentivized by the voluntary carbon market.

Question 3: How can customers use RECs to offset their organizations' CO_2 emissions?

Industry standards divide CO_2 emissions into three scopes.

- Scope 1 covers a company's direct GHG emissions, whether from on-site energy production or other industrial activities.
- Scope 2 covers indirect emissions from energy purchases from off-site facilities.
- Scope 3 covers emissions from employee travel, and embedded energy in furniture and equipment, etc.

The three emission scopes are useful to organize and analyse how an organization is causing GHG emissions; however, the atmosphere doesn't care at all about scopes. The atmosphere only cares about the sum total of all emissions. The less total emissions the better, regardless of within which scope they originated.

Therefore, scopes are *irrelevant* when discussing the purchase of carbon reduction commodities. Any form of commodity that can reliably reduce emissions – call it a Green-e Certified REC, an offset or whatever you like – can be used to zero-out the sum of an organization's emission scopes. No matter what type of offset is chosen by the organization, the emission reduction will occur off site and beyond the direct control of the organization. By its nature, such a commodity is simply unrelated to an organization's scopes. Either buying Green certified RECs or offsets from renewable energy projects puts more renewable energy into the grid and hence reduces carbon emissions, or it does not. If the most cost-effective way to reduce carbon emissions is to transform the electricity grid from coal to wind, why would one not want to incentivize renewable energy projects?

Conclusions

Renewable energy is used all over the world as a mechanism to create carbon offsets. Those offsets are calculated under a variety of national and international standards in this new marketplace. The renewable energy and RECs sold under Green-e rules and the associated CO_2 reductions from those sales are indeed surplus or 'additional' in every meaningful way. Not only are they meaningful, but they have helped and continue to help create a thriving market for renewable energy in the US – a market in which the public should be proud and eager to engage.

RECs to carbon offsets: What's the right exchange rate?

Mark C. Trexler
EcoSecurities

As consumers and companies seek to reduce their carbon footprints with least-cost solutions, the conversion of RECs to carbon offsets (also called GHG offsets) has become increasingly common. In fact, a number of the companies offering to render consumers carbon neutral are actually doing so by purchasing and retiring RECs, as opposed to conventional carbon offsets. How should we feel about that?

The desire to sell RECs into the carbon offset market is a relatively new phenomenon. RECs originally sold for $20–30/MWh when carbon offsets were selling for $2–5/tonne, so there was no incentive to cross markets. Today, however, a rapid expansion of renewable energy capacity has led to lower REC prices, while carbon offset prices have risen. Not surprisingly, REC brokers are eager to sell RECs as carbon offsets at $5–10/tonne, and retail carbon offset providers are selling RECs along with, or instead of, more conventional carbon offsets that might include landfill gas or coal mine methane recovery, reforestation and other kinds of projects (Clean Air-Cool Planet, 2006).

The fundamental question is: do RECs and offsets represent comparable environmental commodities that should be fungible in the same environmental commodity market? RECs and carbon offsets differ in the objectives for which they were created, the actions they represent and the standards by which they are defined. Treating the two as interchangeable in terms of their climate change mitigation impacts is a risky proposition.

Anatomy of an REC

RECs were designed as an accounting instrument for electricity generation from renewable energy sources that would allow consumers to purchase 'renewable electricity' from distant projects. Simply put, ab REC represents a single MWh (megawatt hour) of electricity produced from a qualifying renewable energy technology. Beyond this, however, there is no single definition of what an REC represents. Nearly all definitions of RECs include the 'environmental attributes' created from the generation of the renewable electricity yet fail to establish what these attributes are. These attributes, or benefits, are informally acknowledged to include the reductions in GHG emissions from the production of electricity at a fossil fuel power generating facility. In an efficient marketplace, buyers should have realistic expectations as to what they are getting, which is not the case when poorly defined 'environmental attributes' are included in a commodity.

Currently, RECs are circulated in three markets: (1) the compliance electricity generation market, where electricity generators purchase them to comply with a municipal or state Renewable Portfolio Standard (RPS); (2) the voluntary 'green power' market, in which individuals and organizations purchase RECs because they want to promote renewable energy for personal or Corporate Social Responsibility reasons; and (3) the voluntary GHG offset market, where consumers seeking to go 'carbon neutral' purchase RECs that have been re-branded as carbon offsets. Purveyors of these 'carbon' offsets assure buyers that RECs can be used to offset one's direct and indirect GHG emissions, and at a cheaper price than purchasing traditional carbon offsets.

Compliance market REC purchases to satisfy regulations are relatively straightforward. However, things are more complicated in voluntary markets. Buyers of RECs in the voluntary green power market are seeking to support the expansion of renewable energy. However, it is often not at all clear that their purchase will actually contribute to the construction of new renewable energy facilities. Instead, REC revenues in voluntary markets often end up going to existing renewable energy facilities for which REC funding was not a significant factor in the project's development. In today's market, the question of whether a new wind farm gets built is usually a function of federal tax incentives, rising natural gas prices, and falling technology prices, rather than unpredictable REC sales in the voluntary market. A recent analysis concluded that US investors considering building a new renewable energy facility need a minimum guaranteed revenue stream of $70 to $80 per MWh (Gillenwater, 2007). REC sales in the voluntary market fetch between $1 and $10/MWh and often only guarantee a very short-term (one to five years) revenue stream. As such, REC revenue will usually not materially affect the development of new renewable energy sources. If REC buyers in the voluntary green power market know what they are getting (which is questionable), then the fact that they are funding business-as-usual projects is not necessarily a problem. But when it comes to the voluntary carbon offset market, different rules apply.

RECs purchased as offsets in the voluntary carbon market are assumed to constitute a step towards 'carbon neutrality' for the buyer. Carbon neutrality is an increasingly popular and voluntary means by which individuals and companies are choosing to brand themselves as responsive to global warming and involves inventorying one's footprint, taking internal steps to reduce the footprint, and then purchasing carbon offsets to neutralize the balance. There are several factors that argue against the use of RECs as carbon offsets, most prominent among them the lack of an additionality test for RECs, and the resulting 'business-as-usual' nature of what is usually being purchased.

Anatomy of a carbon offset

A carbon offset is conceptually different from an REC. It represents an action that prevents the emission (or causes the sequestration) of 1 ton of CO_2e (the metric by which different GHGs can be expressed in common units). In order to generate a carbon offset you must first estimate the no-project emissions baseline, calculate the with-project emissions, and quantify the difference (see Figure 3.2, below).

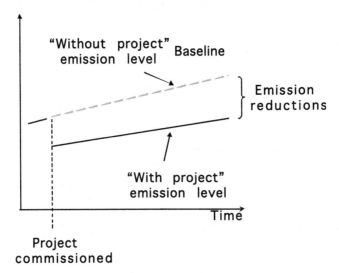

Figure 3.2 *Sample baselines, with and without project occurrence*

The concept of additionality is integral to the function of carbon offsets: an 'additional' emissions reduction is one that would not have occurred in the absence of a market for carbon credits. While the idea of additionality is easy to understand, it can be difficult to measure in practice.

Critics of additionality claim that it is impossible to reliably measure since we're dealing with a counter-factual – namely what would have happened if a project had NOT been built. Indeed, no additionality test can be perfect, but there is no reason that additionality rules cannot be designed that will protect the environmental integrity of carbon markets.

Many kinds of projects can be additional and generate carbon offsets. Additionality is most easy to demonstrate when the only revenue source a project has is carbon offset revenue, but that is by no means a prerequisite. In fact, renewable energy projects can clearly be additional as well. We've worked on solar rural electrification, energy efficiency and other projects in developing countries where one could clearly point to the carbon offset market as the means by which the project was able to proceed. But it's worth noting that these projects can be relatively expensive as carbon offsets.

The trouble with RECs as carbon offsets

RECs, in marked contrast to carbon offsets, do not face additionality requirements. RECs simply represent the generation of renewable energy, regardless of whether the REC market played any role in making that renewable energy project happen. As a result, RECs cannot inherently claim to deliver 'additional' emissions reductions. For buyers looking to reduce their carbon footprint by purchasing offsets, RECs do not provide the same environmental commodity as carbon offsets.

As some purchasers of RECs have grown increasingly sceptical of their purchases, there has been a significant push within the renewable energy community to develop a standard by which to demonstrate the additionality of renewable energy projects and RECs (Elgin, 2007). The Green-e protocol for renewable energy is the foremost example of these efforts, but despite recent fine-tuning, it still treats additionality very weakly (CRS, 2007). The protocol considers additional any renewable energy projects using accepted technologies that aren't required by law, are built after 1 January 2005, and pass a performance test. However, as several organizations pointed out during the public comment period on the Green-e protocol, at least 35 per cent of new renewable energy capacity that came online between 2000 and 2005 that was not built to meet regulatory requirements was also not built to serve the voluntary green power market (Barbour et al, 2007). As such, the protocol's additionality tests leave the door open for selling RECs from renewable energy projects that clearly would have been built anyway.

The right role for RECs

While RECs are not an appropriate substitute for carbon offsets, companies should be able to use them as one component of achieving carbon neutrality. The following example illustrates how RECs and offsets can function in a complementary way in advancing this goal. The example is based on our assumption that coupling an REC with a MWh of fossil fuel electricity effectively renders the fossil fuel electricity carbon-free, an assumption that not everyone may agree with.

Assume that corporation Y has the following characteristics:

- Its Scope 1 (a company's direct GHG emissions, whether from on-site energy production or other industrial activities) emissions total 50,000 tons of CO_2e from on-site energy production and other industrial emissions.
- Its Scope 2 (energy that is purchased from off site) emissions total 100,000 tons based on electricity purchases of 100,000 MWh/year in a coal-dominated electricity grid, with CO_2 emissions of approximately 1 ton per MWh.
- Its Scope 3 inventory (anything from employee travel, to 'upstream' emissions embedded in products purchased or processed by the firm, to 'downstream' emissions associated with transporting and disposing of products sold by the firm) is limited to employee travel and commuting, and totals 20,000 tons of CO_2.

There are many ways the company could make progress towards reducing its carbon footprint, including on-site energy efficiency and renewable energy. With respect to RECs and GHG offsets, corporation Y has the following options:

1   Because the company's GHG inventory totals 170,000 tons of CO_2e, purchasing 170,000 tons of GHG offsets would in principle render company Y carbon neutral.

OR

2   If company Y purchases 100,000 RECs (a 1:1 ratio to its electricity consumption), company Y's GHG inventory totals 70,000 tons instead of 170,000 tons (since the company would have an emissions-free Scope 2). Purchasing 70,000 tons of GHG offsets would then render company Y carbon neutral.

In this example, purchasing more RECs (beyond a 1:1 ratio with electricity consumption) does not further reduce the company's emissions inventory. The company's Scope 2 inventory can be zero if the electricity being purchased has zero emissions; it cannot go negative. Also, in purchasing 100,000 RECs, company Y should not claim to have avoided 100,000 tons of fossil fuel emissions. The company should simply claim credit for having purchased emissions-free electricity, thus rendering its Scope 2 emissions zero.

It's important to note that this approach differs from the way RECs are handled by most inventory protocols. These protocols usually call for the quantification of an emissions footprint for Scope 2 electricity (based on regional CO_2 intensity), followed by the quantification of the emissions footprint for the RECs (based on a regional CO_2 intensity). The latter is then subtracted from the former to generate Scope 2 emissions. This approach was designed to prevent companies with operations around the country from cherry-picking where to apply their RECs (i.e. only facilities in coal-dominated regions). The main problem with this approach is that once RECs are characterized in CO_2 terms, it is almost impossible to prevent companies from arguing that their purchase of RECs displaces or offsets CO_2. Yet such an assertion is misleading and only serves to discredit voluntary and compliance carbon markets.

Conclusions

RECs and carbon offsets are two fundamentally different instruments, created to achieve different goals, governed by different standards, and quantified in different ways. As long as RECs and carbon offsets are kept separate they can peacefully coexist. In fact, REC sales can go a long way in reducing many companies' GHG inventories. But treating RECs and carbon offsets as fungible, when in fact they are quite different commodities, only serves to confuse and undercut the legitimacy and efficiency of the voluntary carbon market.

As REC prices have fallen and carbon offset prices have risen, price-conscious consumers are understandably seduced by the promise of low-cost emission reductions. However, if they're not getting 'additional' reductions for their money, they are being deceived.

Notes

1 The US Department of Energy's Green Power Network offers a current list of companies offering certificate-based green power products: www.eere.energy.gov/greenpower/markets/certificates.shtml?page=2.
2 Renewable energy plants are generally operated as 'must-run', meaning that when (in the case of wind energy) the wind blows, the electricity is accepted into the grid and other resources are 'backed out'. In order for the electric grid to remain stable, there must be approximately equal amounts of energy being fed into the grid by generators and taken out by users.
3 This was also the conclusion of the Northwest Power and Conservation Council staff, based on their Western Electricity Coordinating Council modelling run, which identified the kind of generation displaced, and quantified the GHGs so displaced. Numerous studies from around the US confirm that increasing our use of renewable energy will decrease fossil fuel consumption.

References

Barbour, W. (on behalf of ERT, Pew, CCAR and GHG Experts Network) (2007) 'Joint Comments on the Center for Resource Solutions Draft Green-e Greenhouse Gas Protocol for Renewable Energy. Green-e Climate Protocol for Renewable Energy stakeholder comments', www.ghgnetwork.org/content/article/detail/2090

Bird, L., Kreycik, C. and Friedman, B. (2008) *Green Power Marketing in the United States: A Status Report (Eleventh Edition)*, National Renewable Energy Laboratory, Golden, CO

Carbon Finance (2008) 'CDM approval now impossible to predict', *Carbon Finance Online*, 17 September

Center for Resource Solutions (2006, 2008) Conversation with Andreas Karelas, 8 September 2008 and Green-e Verification Report 2006, www.green-e.org/docs/06Green-e_Verification_Report.pdf

Center for Resource Solutions (2007) *The Green-e Climate Protocol for Renewable Energy* (Version 1.0), Center for Resource Solutions, San Francisco, CA

Center for Resource Solutions (2008) 'Green-e Climate Standards and Governing Documents', www.green-e.org/getcert_ghg_standard.shtml

Clean Air-Cool Planet (2006) 'A Consumer's Guide to Retail Carbon Offset Providers', www.cleanair-coolplanet.org/ConsumersGuidetoCarbonOffsets.pdf

Elgin, B. (2007) 'Little Green Lies: The sweet notion that making a company environmentally friendly can be not just cost-effective but profitable is going up in smoke. Meet the man wielding the torch', *Business Week*, October

Environmental Protection Agency (EPA) (2008) 'Climate Leaders Greenhouse Gas Inventory Protocol Option Modules Methodology for Project Type: Green Power and Renewable Energy Certificates (RECs)', Version 2.1, November 2008, www.epa.gov/climateleaders/documents/greenpower_guidance.pdf

Environmental Resources Trust (ERT) (2006) 'Uniform National Standard for EcoPower Renewable Energy Certificates', June 2006, www.ert.net/pubs/EcoPowerStandard.pdf

Evolution Markets (2007, 2008) Monthly Market Updates, www.evomarkets.com

Gewin, V. (2005) 'What makes energy green? And can it be traded?: Renewable energy and RECs', The Ecosystem Marketplace, www.ecosystemmarketplace.com

Gillenwater, M. (2007) 'Redefining RECs (Part 1): Untangling attributes and offsets', Discussion Paper, Science, Technology and Environmental Policy Program, Princeton University, Princeton, NJ

Rose, T. (2008) 'Looking for carbon in renewable energy', The Ecosystem Marketplace, 7 November, www.ecosystemmarketplace.com

Wiser, R. and Barbose, G. (2008) 'Renewables Portfolio Standards in the United States: A Status Report with Data Through 2007', Lawrence Berkeley National Laboratory, April 2008

Young, T. (2008) 'Companies are falsifying documents in their attempts to gain certification for projects under the clean development mechanism (CDM), according to analyst Point Carbon', *Business Green*, 2 October, www.businessgreen.com/business-green/news/2227429/cdm-applicants-falsifying

4

The Voluntary Carbon Markets:
What the Experts Think

Now that we understand how the voluntary carbon markets function, we are in a position to consider a range of opinions on how they have progressed and how they will operate in the future. Since we are in full agreement with Mark Twain, who once quipped, 'predictions are difficult, especially about the future', we have decided not to make all the predictions ourselves. In this chapter, then, we have asked a series of experts to take a close look at current market trends and to highlight what they feel are the current critical issues facing the voluntary carbon markets.

The following editorials represent a wide range of perspectives, and sometimes conflicting opinions, from a variety of market players and experts. Read on to find out what scientists and investors, project developers and policy makers, communities and corporations, and retailers and conservationists think about the voluntary carbon markets of today and tomorrow.

An economist's perspective on the voluntary carbon markets: Useful but not sufficient

Janet Peace
Pew Center on Global Climate Change

When trying to understand the relationship between regulated carbon markets, voluntary carbon markets and the larger global fight against climate change, it is important to bear in mind two things: (1) voluntary efforts alone, although important, will not sufficiently reduce greenhouse gas (GHG) emissions; and (2) since the US is the largest emitter of these gases, accounting for approximately 21 per cent of global emissions, no meaningful regulatory effort can succeed without the entire country's involvement. Luckily, both of these seem to be gaining widespread acknowledgement – at least at the state level and increasingly with Congress as well.[1] Bearing these facts in mind, we can now turn to look at

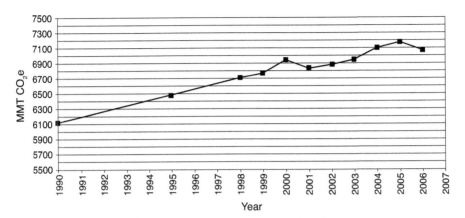

Figure 4.1 *US GHG emissions growth*

Note: Emissions grown = 16% 1990–2006
Source: Energy Information Administration (EIA), 2007

what is happening in the US vis-à-vis carbon markets, and voluntary carbon markets in particular.

The voluntary markets for carbon have dramatically increased in the last few years. Market participants now include project developers, consumers, firms preparing for mandatory state or regional regulatory programmes, several registries and even a couple of trading exchanges. Without a mandatory federal programme that imposes specific and consistent reduction requirements throughout all sectors of our economy, however, the current, developing GHG market may not have enough demand, supply, consistency or infrastructure to fully address the challenge we face from climate change.

It is clear that voluntary efforts are not enough because we have had a voluntary programme in the US now for over a decade and emissions continue to rise at an alarming rate. Since 1990 they have increased about 16 per cent, even though President Bush established a voluntary emissions intensity target in 2002 which aimed to reduce the average emissions per unit of output in our economy 18 per cent by 2012.

Although incapable of achieving the levels of emission cuts needed, voluntary markets are important and can aid in addressing the challenge of climate change in a number of ways. First, they can act as an important precursor to a mandatory emissions trading programme by educating stakeholders (including policy makers and firms) about emission reduction opportunities, measurement tools and infrastructure requirements. Industry also benefits from learning about trading and risk management in a voluntary market because prices are likely lower than they would be under a mandatory system. The Chicago Climate Exchange (CCX) provides a good example of this. CCX specifically promotes membership by noting that participation builds 'the practical skills needed to manage and trade GHG emissions', and it is noteworthy that participants have typically paid less than $5 per metric ton of CO_2 since CCX began operating (CCX, 2007).

In addition to being a precursor for compliance markets, voluntary markets can also act as a significant complement to any mandatory programme. For instance, where voluntary reductions are certified as offsets that can be used towards compliance in a cap-and-trade programme, they help increase market depth and liquidity (by increasing the number of suppliers who can provide supply when needed). The use of offsets in a mandatory market also broadens the financial incentive for innovation to firms not covered by regulations, and can provide an important mechanism for containing the costs associated with meeting mandatory targets (EPA, 2008).[2] In addition, the general public can participate in a voluntary market by purchasing offsets to cover their own GHG emissions – again further expanding the scope of trading beyond that of a mandatory programme and educating consumers about the importance of their own emissions and actions. The Climate Trust and TerraPass, for example, are two organizations that offer individuals the ability to buy GHG offsets to compensate for their travel-related emissions.

And, while there is much discussion in this book and elsewhere on the relationship between mandatory and voluntary carbon markets, in my view, implementation of a mandatory programme with targets and clearly defined rules will only improve and could potentially even expand the voluntary markets. Individuals and firms will likely have more confidence that carbon offsets (whether for the voluntary or regulatory market) represent real reductions when rules, standards and reporting requirements provide a framework to judge quality. Furthermore, mandatory and voluntary programmes can and do operate together as evidenced by the significant volume of voluntary transactions in Europe – home to the largest mandatory GHG emissions trading programme in the world. According to the *State of the Voluntary Carbon Markets 2008* report (Hamilton et al, 2008), the EU accounts for 47 per cent of buyer transactions in the voluntary markets.

Credibility is a vital issue for all carbon markets and its significance cannot be overstated. Without some level of consumer understanding and confidence that emissions trading is not a shell game, there is little chance of developing the political will necessary to set up a large-scale mandatory GHG trading system, let alone a trading system that would implement a broad-based offsets programme to incentivize emission reductions from sectors outside of those capped directly by the programme.

Consistent definitions and protocols for specific types of emission reduction activities would help buyers (and ultimately sellers) of voluntary reductions understand what they are buying, in much the same way that the Energy Star label in the US has helped consumers recognize and select energy-efficient appliances. This need for consistency and credibility has been recognized by participants in the voluntary market, including CCX, World Resources Institute, the Climate Group, Climate Wedge, the California Climate Action Registry (CCAR), and others who have attempted to create a credible definition. To date, however, the definition of an offset is still not uniform and buyers must closely scrutinize the quality of their carbon purchases.

So where does this leave us? What will happen by 2010? Will the carbon market be truly global? While this is desirable, it is unlikely since 2010 is only one year away. By then we may first see development of several new regulated carbon markets in several regions throughout the US, and these may or may not be linked to each other. Over time (and how long this time frame will be is hard to say), these regional markets will likely be expanded or rolled into a national programme, and some time after that, this national market may establish close links with international markets. However the carbon markets develop, one thing is clear: a mandatory programme is necessary for the development of a fully functioning carbon market. And while voluntary efforts are useful, they should be seen only as a precursor and complement to regulated markets, never as a substitute. Alone they will never be a sufficient remedy to the problem of global climate change.

A conservationist's perspective on the voluntary carbon markets: Can they help us overcome inertia?

Ben Vitale
Conservation International

Climate change is such a dire problem that if we are to tackle it, optimism, entrepreneurial innovation, steadfast conviction and systematic changes in global social and economic infrastructure must be combined in amounts never before orchestrated. We need the visionary oversight of policy makers, the innovation of the private sector and the hope and conviction of all global citizens.

By putting a price on the activities that lead to climate change, carbon markets can help knit together the activities of businesses, consumers and policy makers on all sides of the world. Unfortunately, deploying global policy takes decades, and will only be effective when all countries and individuals adopt the most stringent GHG reduction targets. Today's compliance markets do not come close to substantially reducing the potential impacts of dangerous levels of climate change at or below the 400 parts per million (ppm) CO_2 that many scientists advise, although recent commitments to reduce emissions at least 50 per cent by 2050 begin to make a more earnest attempt.

Recent occurrences are ringing alarm bells. For example, studies project that summer Arctic sea ice may disappear altogether within a decade, thus drastically altering natural marine food chains and further endangering animals such as the polar bear. Mankind's food production in many impoverished arid areas may be impacted by dramatically altered rain and weather patterns which in some recent examples have reduced the food security of already vulnerable communities.

Voluntary carbon markets have an important role to play in the coming years. As we enter a transition period between lax regulation and the sort of drastic reductions that are needed to address climate change, voluntary markets can move us to adopt innovative climate change solutions more quickly and flexibly, especially in the forest sector.

Voluntary markets are not as constrained as the regulated markets, so a key role for these markets should be to push innovation and fund creative solutions ahead of, and in addition to, regulation. Projects funded by the voluntary market must be of high quality and they must deliver measurable emissions reductions, but this does not necessarily mean that only regulated modalities should be considered. For example, the current compliance markets place land-use projects at a disadvantage by excluding the emissions that result from deforestation completely, disallowing forest-based credits from the largest emission trading market, and by limiting the amount of land-use-based credits that countries may use for compliance.

Sir Nicholas Stern and other experts have clearly and effectively argued that dangerous levels of GHG concentrations cannot be avoided without considering the approximately 20 per cent of annual emissions resulting from deforestation and other land-use change. In addition, recent progress has been made by the United Nations Framework Convention on Climate Change (UNFCCC) to address the technical, policy and financial incentives needed to include these emissions credits in a new compliance framework.

In these intervening years before international, post-Kyoto rules for avoided deforestation are clear, strongly supporting 'Reducing Emissions from Deforestation and Degradation' (REDD) and substantial forest restoration projects allows the voluntary carbon markets to yield many simultaneous benefits. These include:

- time to pursue alternative technology and development pathways in the short term because forest-based emission reductions can be generated relatively quickly;
- support for global goals to protect threatened biological diversity noted in the Convention on Biological Diversity (CBD), the Ramsar Convention on Wetlands of International Importance and the Convention on the Conservation of Migratory Species of Wild Animals;
- a new revenue source for impoverished developing countries and communities that are forest carbon- and biodiversity-rich;
- opportunities to contribute to poverty alleviation by furthering the Millennium Development Goals (MDGs) assuming carbon credit prices produce sufficient incentives compared to alternative land uses.

This emphasis on tangible projects accruing multiple benefits (i.e. carbon emission reductions, biodiversity conservation and community livelihoods) with broad stakeholder engagement is particularly important because climate change is occurring during, and contributing to, the sixth-largest species extinction spasm ever documented.

There are many multiple-benefit projects that must sell both compliance and voluntary carbon credits in order to be financially viable. One such project is Conservation International's Ankeniheny-Zahamena Corridor Restoration and Protection Project in Madagascar (see Box 4.1). This project seeks to produce Kyoto CDM certified emissions reductions and voluntary emissions reductions produced by avoiding the burning of tropical forest, as well as biodiversity protection and sustainable community livelihoods. The project expects to obtain as much as one-third to one-half of the required project financing from the marketing of carbon credits.

Madagascar is scaling up efforts to reduce deforestation, and recent analyses conducted by the government of Madagascar and Conservation International documented an eightfold reduction in deforestation nationally since the 1990s. This result is globally significant because it demonstrates that reductions can be achieved at a national scale while addressing potential project-based leakage. If both the voluntary and compliance markets move swiftly to mobilize hundreds of millions of dollars for this class of emission reductions, then the permanence of Madagascar's and other countries' forest carbon credits can be assured.

The government has made progress by bestowing provisional protected area status on the entire corridor area. The seven Malagasy implementing partners have begun restoring native forest, selecting from over 90 native species of trees, and gaining new scientific and silviculture knowledge for use in future restoration programmes. The project will be the first large-scale REDD project to apply the new methodology developed by the World Bank with input from CATIE, Winrock International, Terra Carbon, and Conservation International. These innovations will be used as a foundation to scale-up REDD activities both in Madagascar and in other countries.

Many other sovereign countries are developing national programmes to reduce emissions from deforestation and degradation. Each country has different national circumstances, forest cover, historical and future emissions profiles, and solutions to effectively protect forests, peatlands and other key ecosystems that could be sources of emissions. For example, Guyana's President Bharrat Jagdeo has offered to protect Guyana's entire forest estate in exchange for adequate financial incentives that contribute to Guyana's low carbon economy investments. The government of Liberia is pursuing a forest reform strategy that integrates community, conservation and commercial activities that expect to maintain current forest cover for future generations. The voluntary carbon markets can provide immediate incentives for demonstration activities that provide tangible benefits for communities and conservation while simultaneously informing policy makers.

In addition to opening up carbon finance to REDD, voluntary markets also have a unique role to play in heightening public awareness of climate change, its threats and its solutions. The world needs action and commitment – in other words, sacrifice – from citizens on a scale not experienced in many decades, if ever. Citizens innately understand the significant value of forests and success stories in the voluntary markets help people understand what happens 'there' – in other parts of the world – is felt 'everywhere'. The voluntary markets, when coupled with strict regulation, can help drive the early action, entrepreneurial innovation, increased consumer awareness and engagement necessary to stabilize GHG concentrations in the atmosphere. In particular, voluntary markets can help citizens in developed countries understand how they might assist those communities in developing countries that are especially vulnerable to the impacts of climate change.

Box 4.1 Case Study:
Ankeniheny–Zahamena Corridor Restoration and Protection Project, Republic of Madagascar

The Ankeniheny–Zahamena Corridor Restoration and Protection Project is conducting native forest restoration and protection activities with two primary goals:
1 To establish natural forest corridors that allow viable biological connectivity among several currently isolated high biodiversity forests and protected areas; and
2 To promote sustainable cultivation systems to increase soil fertility, protect watersheds, and stabilize land use to reduce deforestation in the 425,000 hectare corridor.

These activities will significantly increase forest cover and reduce deforestation, sequestering and avoiding approximately 17 million tons of CO_2. They are being carried out in conjunction with local communities, government agencies and other stakeholders. Specific actions include:

- increasing forest cover by avoiding deforestation, reconnecting the fragmented landscape, and restoring degraded lands to functional ecosystems;
- developing new agricultural and forestry techniques to improve productivity of degraded zones and provide new alternatives to farmers and communities;
- building local capacity in Madagascar to implement climate change initiatives including technical, implementation, financial and legal aspects;
- promoting project benefits to (1) purchasers of compliance and voluntary emissions reductions who provide project financing, and (2) donors and funding agencies interested in supporting community livelihoods and biodiversity conservation benefit;
- using proven methodologies, monitoring techniques, remote sensing and aerial photography to assess forest change at a national level.

Growing voluntary markets in a regulated world

While voluntary markets are an important means of combating climate change for all of the reasons just cited, they should in no way be seen as an alternative to regulation. For this reason, some argue that voluntary markets are superfluous and that they will cease to exist once regulated markets emerge.

If global and regional regulations provided a completely closed system capable of accounting for global emissions from all sources, these critics of voluntary markets would probably be right. Regulatory markets would displace voluntary markets or, at least, reduce them dramatically. This scenario, however, is not likely to become a reality for at least another few decades, and it may never happen.

Even if countries like the US implemented carbon cap-and-trade schemes tomorrow, the regulations guiding these schemes would probably be limited in scope, leaving many emitting sectors out of the market. This is certainly the case with the Lieberman–Warner legislation introduced in the US Congress in 2008. And if the regulated markets become very fragmented – with each country adopting its own rules – then the line may blur between the voluntary and regulated markets. For these reasons, the voluntary market may not peak for a decade or more depending on the level of limits and breadth of solutions established by global climate change regulation and resulting compliance markets.

Whatever happens in the next decade, it is probably safe to say that the voluntary carbon markets will be larger in 2020 than they are now. Since the magnitude of global climate change is so large, and the current pace of policy interventions is so slow, voluntary carbon markets could continue transacting hundreds of millions of dollars annually before truly effective compliance carbon markets are up and running at the scale required to avoid dangerous climate change.

In the meantime, governments are developing innovative bilateral or multilateral agreements outside traditional emissions trading markets that may boost investments in projects that might be considered 'voluntary'. For example, Australia, Norway and Germany are allocating hundreds of millions of dollars annually to developing countries to reduce emissions from deforestation and other land-use change immediately. This is only a short-term measure, but these allocations signal the required urgency and lend further credence to the idea that perhaps the voluntary carbon markets can fill more of the gap between existing markets and the needed emissions reductions in the short term. These actions also call into question whether market or non-market mechanisms will be more effective at addressing climate change, and which solution will provide sufficient incentives to reduce emissions quickly. Already some Brazilian states are establishing funding mechanisms and programmes to reduce emissions from deforestation. Marriott and Bradesco are supporting these early efforts to protect forests in the state of Amazonas, and others are likely to follow across numerous countries in the Amazon region.

In a similar vein, multilateral agencies such as the World Bank are strengthening their position in the compliance market while amassing significant new funds for technology transfer and forest protection, which may affect the voluntary carbon markets. Of particular noteworthiness are the World Bank's Forest Carbon Partnership Fund and the Strategic Climate Fund. Conversely, these bilateral and multilateral annual expenditures are many times the size of the currently global voluntary markets' financial value, so they may bias the size and/or types of projects marketing credits into the voluntary carbon markets. The effects of dramatically increased bilateral agency, multilateral agency and developing country funding on the voluntary carbon markets may be a key trend to watch in the near future.

Meanwhile, these mechanisms might provide significant opportunities for consumers, institutions and non-regulated businesses to take voluntary action in ways that grow the market. Clearly, governments, scientists and the private sector must continually search for new ways to unlock creativity and entrepreneurship to address climate change quickly. Governments need to enact climate legislation, but they must also provide incentives to help speed the adoption of new lower-emissions technologies and activities. Businesses are quickly learning how they can become climate friendly while turning a profit. For example, some leadership companies such as ST Microelectronics, DuPont, Ricoh Corporation, Dell, HSBC, Swiss Re, Starbucks and others have already taken on voluntary commitments that go beyond their regulated obligations. Many financial services firms are supporting activities in the voluntary markets – particularly in the US – to gain a foothold before compliance markets are launched, and to complement European, Japanese and Australian compliance efforts.

Change, it seems, is happening, but it needs to happen more quickly and on a larger scale. Fortunately, there is room for hope: when John Doerr and Vinod Khosla – the venture capitalists who first backed global giants such as Google and Sun Microsystems – and other investors begin funding new green technologies to deploy in the growing economies of India, China and Brazil as well as the industrialized countries, it is a strong signal that the gloves have come off, and entrepreneurs are ready to begin developing solutions that make both commercial and environmental sense in this carbon-constrained world.

A project developer's perspective on the voluntary carbon markets: Carbon sequestration in the Sierra Gorda of Mexico

David Patrick Ross and Martha Isabel Ruiz Corzo
Bosque Sustentable

Located in a transition zone between the Nearctic and Neotropical biogeographical regions, the Sierra Gorda Biosphere Reserve is the most ecosystem-diverse natural protected area in Mexico. The 15 vegetation types found within the Reserve's boundaries include semi-desert scrub, temperate forests of pines and oaks, cloud forests, dry tropical forests and tropical rain forests. Ranking second among Mexico's natural protected areas in terms of biodiversity, the Sierra Gorda is home to multiple species of Mexican felines including the jaguar, puma, bobcat, margay, ocelot and jaguarundi.

Despite its natural riches, the Reserve – located in the Sierra Madre Oriental mountain range in the state of Queretaro – is an area of severe poverty. Approximately 100,000 inhabitants live in 638 localities throughout the Reserve's 383,567 hectares (32 per cent of the state's territory), and four of the five municipalities are ranked as highly marginalized. The fifth is ranked as very highly marginalized. More than 70 per cent of the economically active population in Pinal de Amoles, a site in Sierra Gorda that sources carbon sequestration credits for the UN Foundation, make less than US$8.00 per day.

Bosque Sustentable, A.C., a non-governmental organization founded in 2002, works in close coordination with Sierra Gorda Biosphere Reserve and its civil society partner organization, Grupo Ecologico Sierra Gorda. From 1998 to 2004 the organizations of the Sierra Gorda focused their carbon efforts on looking for opportunities to enter the carbon market created by the Kyoto Protocol. In March 2006, we signed a contract with the United Nations Foundation for the sale of 5230 emission reduction units (tCO2e) from the Reserve. The contract was the culmination of years of hard work, and our experience with the international carbon market during this time highlights the difficulties and opportunities for organizations interested in developing carbon sequestration projects in areas of poverty.

An uphill battle

The barriers we encountered when trying to enter the Clean Development Mechanism (CDM) of Kyoto are common to many areas of poverty located in Mexico and throughout Latin America. At the most basic level, they include the lack of capital for developing projects, and the lack of forest management skills among local landholders. Even when local capacity has been developed, high costs for verification and certification of emission reductions can result in more carbon money going into the hands of consultants from other countries than to local people planting and protecting trees.

Another important barrier is the pattern of land ownership in the Sierra Gorda, which lacks large, uninterrupted properties. Bosque Sustentable works with small landholders with an average plantation size of 1 hectare. This means that for a project of 500 hectares – small by international standards – Bosque Sustentable must work with approximately 500 different landholders scattered throughout the mountains. These properties lack telephone services and are accessible only by hours of driving on rough, unpaved roads, dramatically increasing the per-unit costs of carbon sequestration. In addition, the majority of landholders do not hold title to the property in their own name. In most cases, the title to the property is in the name of a deceased relative and although possession is not in dispute, legal costs and exorbitant notary fees prevent the landholders from updating the titles.

Not surprisingly, impoverished farmers require payments in the early years of the plantations, prior to the onset of sustainable harvesting. Although government programmes support tree planting, project mortality is high, and the payments are increasingly insufficient to attract participation. Carbon sales provide an additional incentive for participation in the form of small payments to landholders who otherwise simply cannot afford the investment of time and resources to establish and ensure the survival of a plantation. Although some buyers in the CDM market will make up-front investments, the additional risk involved usually entails a lower purchase price.

The unresolved issue of additionality was also difficult for us to navigate as a community project in a rural area. With the support of an international consultant with CDM experience, Bosque Sustentable argues that although its project includes lands located within a federal Natural Protected Area (NPA), the lands are private and there is no legal requirement for reforestation; therefore, the CDM requirement for project additionality can be met. Other consultants and certain non-governmental organizations, however, continue to argue that reforestation within NPAs should not be considered 'additional' for CDM purposes.

For these reasons and others, Bosque Sustentable and its partner organizations decided to abandon their efforts to enter the CDM market. In the words of Martha Isabel Ruiz Corzo, Director of the Sierra Gorda Biosphere Reserve, 'For years we heard that the Clean Development Mechanism was a tool for sustainable development, but the reality is that the CDM is light years away from the needs of areas of poverty.'

A better fit

Now Bosque Sustentable is focusing on the voluntary carbon markets. Its programme of Carbon Sequestration for Sustainable Forestry in the Sierra Gorda Biosphere Reserve is targeted to organizations, businesses and individuals that not only want to contribute to the fight against global warming, but also want to fight poverty and conserve biodiversity.

The Sierra Gorda carbon sequestration project, developed with the assistance of Woodrising Consulting, Inc and the 'Biodiversity Conservation in the Sierra Gorda Biosphere Reserve' project (supported by the Global Environment Facility), sequesters carbon by reforesting lands previously converted to agricultural and livestock uses in the Sierra Gorda Biosphere Reserve and its area of influence in the state of San Luis Potosi. The project fights poverty through the creation of numerous small-scale landholder-managed plantations. Participants include private and communal landowners, as well as landholders for whom there is no dispute regarding possession (as indicated by a record of possession obtained from the local municipal authority). All participants must sign contracts committing to the management of their plantations for carbon sequestration for 30 years and transferring the legal right to emission reductions to Bosque Sustentable.

The sale of emission reductions provides the financial incentives needed to obtain and maintain landowner participation until the plantations reach sufficient maturity to provide the landowners with income from sustainable harvesting. These incentives are backed by a coordinated effort, implemented by a team of community organizers and forestry experts, to organize the landowners into well-equipped professional associations that provide them with professional training on silvicultural techniques, sustainable forestry management, wood transformation technologies, product development and marketing, and business management. The project preserves old-growth forests by discouraging their use for wood and instead makes regulated plantations the primary source of wood for the region.

As structured, the project requires up-front payments from buyers for the sequestration of carbon during a project life of 30 years. Emission reduction credits are issued every five years following verification. Although specific properties are identified for each individual sale of emissions reductions, Bosque Sustentable maintains the flexibility to substitute emission reductions from similar properties as needed. In addition, Bosque Sustentable retains 20 per cent of the projected emissions reductions as a form of self-insurance called a 'project buffer'.

The sale to the UN Foundation of 5230 emission reduction credits is the first for the project. As part of its commitment to carbon neutral operations, the UN Foundation used the methodology of the WRI/WBCSD GHG Protocol and tools provided by the World Resources Institute to calculate the total amount of its historical CO_2 emissions from electricity consumption, heating and cooling, and air travel of employees at its Washington DC and New York offices. With pro bono legal services generously proved by Baker & McKenzie, the UN Foundation then purchased an equivalent amount of carbon offsets from Bosque Sustentable, which received the assistance of the Mexican Center for Environmental Law.

The Sierra Gorda experience shows that the voluntary carbon markets have the potential to play an important role in sustainable development efforts around the world. To achieve this potential, however, the development of rigid Kyoto-like standards for the voluntary markets must be avoided. Instead, flexible but reliable criteria should be utilized to meet the needs of areas of severe poverty.

An NGO's perspective on the voluntary carbon markets: Key to solving the problem

Ben Henneke
Clean Air Cool Planet

As all nations, and even all energy companies, now accept that climate change is real and actions need to be taken, it is time to get serious about how to accomplish the enormous challenge we face. It is no longer enough for policy makers to posture, to blame the problem on big polluters, to do studies and analysis, and to continue the nearly endless debates about giving away allowances versus auctioning them. It is now time for all of us to get busy doing something about the problem.

The only way to get busy and get serious about the climate change problem is to harness voluntary actions everywhere, from the largest company to the smallest African village. It is going to take billions of voluntary actions by people in forests and farms as well as in factories and cities.

The good news is that voluntary actions are easy, fast and usually cheap!

Unfortunately, today's regulators and regulatory discussions are either focusing on the big emitters – big oil, big industry, big utilities, big cement – or chasing after wonderful technologies – like hydrogen or fuel cells – that will take 10 to 30 years before they can impact the world's economies. By aiming at the wrong targets and trying the wrong techniques, policy makers continue to ensure failure at addressing the whole problem.

Let's look at the sources being discussed today. Power plants all over the world represent 20–24 per cent of the carbon emissions, and there are few technologies for dramatically increasing efficiency or reducing their carbon footprints. Even the hoped-for solution of 'carbon sequestration' is a daunting technical and political task that is at least one decade and probably two decades away from making a dent in power plant emissions. So, even if we had the political will to cut emissions directly from the power sector by one-third (a nearly impossible technical and engineering task under current conditions), we would only be able to reduce GHGs by 6 or 7 per cent. This is not nearly enough, not even 10 per cent of what is needed.

Which sector has the most untapped potential? Land-based sequestration – reduced deforestation, reforestation, and agricultural sequestration. These strategies have been largely neglected in policy debates, yet deforestation and agriculture account for 33–40 per cent of all GHGs emitted. Deforestation alone accounts for 20–21 per cent.

The forestry sector even has the potential to go from contributing to the global problem to becoming the biggest solution to the problem. Proper incentives for forestry could mean a 30 per cent change in GHG emissions by eliminating deforestation and reforesting at half the rate we have been destroying the forests. Reforestation can create dramatic, real carbon sinks, create benefits to the people who live in or near the forest and improve water supplies to those in the cities. Reforestation can decrease poverty, create jobs and encourage economic development all at the same time.

So, if we're going to solve the climate change problem, billions of people must take voluntary action, and those actions must stop deforestation and rapidly repair the damage done over the last 50 years. And the only way to get billions of people to do anything is for them to do it voluntarily – to give them the moral, personal, civic and the financial incentives to start taking actions that heal the planet.

We need to use all the methods of persuasion known to humankind that result in voluntary action. Churches and synagogues and mosques and temples should become hotbeds of encouragement for reforestation and changed lifestyles. Schools and town offices and city halls should be sources of accurate information and visible leadership.

And, oh yes, we need a functioning market. A voluntary market.

Whether through barter, clamshells or debit cards, mankind has been using voluntary markets to improve both physical and psychological quality of life for thousands of years. Experience shows that markets increase choice, create abundance, develop technology and create 'win–win' situations for both buyer and seller. Real markets develop where there is actual demand, and freedom to meet that demand in a number of ways.

Regulatory markets are different. Regulatory markets are a variation of 'rationing' programmes tried in many countries during World Wars I and II. In those times, the market portion was called a 'black market'. But late 20th century economists suggested using this rationing approach and making the market a key feature, rather than a violation of the rationing programme. Regulatory markets are new, relatively untested and, unfortunately, have a pretty spotty history so far.

For example, the pilot EU ETS carbon market suffered a market crash in 2007 when it was discovered that the governments had given away many more EUAs (allowances) than the operating facilities under the 'cap' needed. Especially at the pilot scale there are numerous examples of market failures. In fact, each regulatory market keeps treading the same well-worn path of giving out too many allowances. Whether the South Coast of California, the US SOx or NOx programmes, or now the RGGI carbon programme in the northeastern US, the regulatory/political process just has not been able to avoid handing out too many allowances.

Regulatory markets have also failed to provide a reliable 'cost of compliance' as originally expected. For example, over the past decade, US sulphur dioxide market (SOx) prices have varied over 1500 per cent while the nitrous oxide (N_2O) market has fluctuated by over 300 per cent and the California RECLAIM programme set a record by moving over 120,000 per cent! I am sure that the 'cost of compliance' exists somewhere in those wild swings of prices – but it's not of very much use in actually making good long-term environmental and economic decisions.

That kind of volatility doesn't happen in voluntary markets. Even the US stock market crashes of 1939 and 1987 only showed fluctuations of 24 per cent.

Voluntary markets, which I deem 'real markets', are determined by real demand and voluntary supply. Real markets are characterized by hundreds of choices on how to meet that demand. Look in any automobile dealership, any drug store or any supermarket to see the enormous number of supply choices that a real market will provide to meet the customer's demand. In real markets suppliers and buyers also look different from each other. Farmers are different from supermarkets and supermarkets are different from customers who go there to buy food.

But regulatory markets so far have all looked the same, the same large industrial sources. 'Round up the usual suspects' has been the policy maker's cry. This 'sameness' is especially true of the utility industry. All of them buy fuel, all of them make electricity. They have very few independent choices on how to reduce their emissions of carbon. And their 'customers' have very little real choice about what they can use in lieu of electricity.

Lack of choice and lack of flexibility in regulatory markets have big costs, create big political fights, and thus big delays in addressing the global problems. In these last few years we have seen dramatic evidence of the cost of governments making the wrong market design choices. We have seen the project-based 'voluntary market' create dozens of methodologies and project approaches that have the capacity to scale up dramatically and impact global outcomes. And we have seen the EU ETS programme disclose high prices for big industry to shrink their footprint even a few per cent. But bad policy choices erected trade barriers against project-based tons in the EU ETS that are costing European nations billions of dollars, and sending the rest of the world a false signal about the cost to solve the climate change problem.

At the same time, the voluntary market participants are often starving for capital, unable to expand as rapidly as their potential would suggest because they are excluded from the regulatory market. This is crazy. Let's remember that even if all of the European industries cut their emissions dramatically, it would have a small impact on the global problem. But if millions and then billions of people around the world can access the carbon market to pay them to take voluntary actions, they can have an enormous impact on the global problem.

So, how should we make regulatory markets work better? Here are some basic suggestions:

1   Use the regulatory market cap to create substantial and increasing demand by issuing a declining number of allowances. This means giving (or auctioning) many fewer allowances than the sources presently use.
2   Give the industries inside the cap more flexibility to make reductions inside or outside of their fenceline. This gives them the ability to look for lower-cost carbon credits to accomplish the desired environmental results.
3   Rapidly move to include transportation and other presently unregulated sectors into the carbon emissions reduction process. This can probably be most easily done by putting a carbon tax on the use of fossil fuel, but with the right for people to use carbon credits to pay the tax.
4   Use the existing CDM, VCS, CCBA and Gold Standard quality control procedures to create carbon credits.
5   Develop the governmental capacity to review and audit the quality of offset credits being used for compliance. This can be done inside each nation's income tax function or through a separate bureaucracy.
6   Use the World Trade Organization's already established judicial procedures to take care of any major market imperfections caused by lack of international cooperation.

A properly designed regulatory market will create real demand and create it quickly. Industries will look for high quality projects that can reduce their carbon footprint more cheaply or more rapidly than they are able to do inside their fenceline. New equipment and new technologies will be developed and sold to reduce the industrial, real estate or transportation carbon emissions tax or allowance burden.

We will also see an explosion in voluntary actions taken by millions, and then billions of people to reduce their own carbon footprint and to supply this newly created market for carbon reductions. There will be all kinds of supply – not just wind power projects, or methane destruction projects, or industrial gas destruction projects – but an amazing array of voluntary actions and new ideas.

I believe we will see the kind of astonishing variety and regular improvement in quality of carbon credits that we have seen in almost all consumer products in the last 50 years. Some, like credits from the International Small Group & Tree Planting Program, will help impoverished farmers in the developing world create better local environments and have a new 'cash crop' in the form of forest carbon. Some will find ways to help impoverished city dwellers, some will find ways to help improve soil quality through carbon sequestration, and some will find ways to make and package products with less environmental impact.

What all these people, methodologies and technologies need is demand. The policy maker's job is to create that predictable demand. They must create the demand through shortage of allowances and a tax or tax-like price impact that will allow people to rationally change their behaviours to reduce their emissions of GHGs and seek ways to sequester carbon. Then we can celebrate the diversity and the quantity of the voluntary responses.

This is today's opportunity for the voluntary carbon markets: to unleash individual initiative now and create the systemic innovation and widespread participation that will allow billions of people to participate in the carbon markets in the next decades.

Let's get to work.

A retailer's perspective on the voluntary carbon markets: A vital complement to regulation

Bill Sneyd and Jonathan Shopley
The CarbonNeutral Company

The CarbonNeutral Company sold its first credit in 1997, and since then developments have taken the voluntary carbon sector from a potentially short-lived fad on the fringes of serious action on climate change to its rightful place as a critically important and effective response which is needed to complement heavy handed and slow regulatory responses. Some of the key changes that have taken place over the past several years include:

- Massive growth in the value of carbon traded on the voluntary market.
- Governments' support of voluntary action as a complement to regulation – for example:
  - The UK government has started to offset the emissions from its own travel and has committed that the central government estate will be carbon neutral by 2012.
  - The Japanese government has developed guidance on voluntary offset activities.
  - The French government agency, ADEME, has developed a portal for voluntary offsetting including a 'charter' and details of companies that have committed to meeting the charter.
  - The Norwegian government has committed Norway to becoming carbon neutral by 2050 through a combination of reductions and offsetting.
- Carbon credit standards in the voluntary market have started to grow up.
- A self-regulatory body for entities serving the voluntary market – International Carbon Reduction and Offset Alliance (ICROA) – has been

formed. Members have committed to bringing their businesses into compliance with its code of best practice.

Despite these developments, it has not all been smooth sailing for voluntary offsetting. Some critics believe that offsets should not count in company claims of emissions reductions, and other organizations believe that carbon neutral claims need to be regulated for the sake of consumer protection.

The Carbon Trust, a company set up by the UK government to accelerate the transition to a low carbon economy, recently launched a Carbon Reduction Standard that explicitly excludes the use of offsets in claiming emissions reductions. According to the press release that accompanied the launch of the Standard, 'Unlike other award schemes, it requires organisations to take action themselves rather than paying others to reduce via off-setting – a practice seen as credible by only one in ten consumer respondents in a recent Carbon Trust study.'

The UK Advertising Standards Authority (ASA) and the US Federal Trade Commission (FTC) have each spent months investigating complaints regarding carbon neutral claims. And, the US state of California contemplated two separate bills that sought to regulate the voluntary carbon market. Although the complaints have largely been dismissed and the bills didn't pass, their very existence could be seen as reinforcing the consumer mistrust quoted by the Carbon Trust above.

Given the mixed picture that we have painted – with improvements to both the structure of the voluntary market and carbon instruments on the one hand, and continued challenges to the very concept of offsetting from government, media and some NGOs – we think it is worth restating the role that the voluntary carbon market can and must play.

The prevailing scientific and economic consensus reflected in the IPCC's 4th Assessment Report (2007) and the Stern Report (2007) is that an absolute reduction of 60–80 per cent in global GHG emissions is required by mid-century to prevent material damage to the world's economy. If anything, the scientific position is hardening, with the consensus moving towards the upper end of this range.

There is little evidence, however, that current international negotiations will put us onto the required trajectory. The EU (the region with slowest emissions growth under a business-as-usual scenario) looks set to take a lead by committing to a 20–30 per cent reduction by 2020, but the regions where most emissions growth is likely to come from – China and India – seem very unlikely to take on an absolute emissions cap immediately post-2012; and, while everyone expects some change in the US position following the presidential election, it would be naive to expect dramatic reductions to be delivered in the short term. In the version of this chapter we submitted two years ago, we stated:

> *Only the expansion of the voluntary carbon market has the capacity to bypass the naturally cumbersome progress of a regulatory approach and make up the difference between regulated reductions, which on their own will be too little too late.*

Progress in international negotiations over the last two years has not changed this view.

So, in recent years, the foundations for a massively more effective voluntary carbon market have been laid, but proponents of the voluntary carbon markets need to win the arguments surrounding the value of offsetting so that voluntary action can step up to the challenge of delivering gigatonnes of reductions.

To that end we would like to address some of the common myths or challenges that are thrown at offset-based carbon management.

Myth #1: An 'offset' is not as good as a reduction

This myth stems from a fundamental misunderstanding about what an 'offset' is, and the terminology used in the voluntary market does not help. An offset *is* an emissions reduction. The CDM got things right by naming its carbon instrument a Certified Emission Reduction (CER). A carbon credit or 'offset' – providing it has met agreed quality assurance standards – represents a reduction in emissions against a documented business-as-usual or baseline scenario. In our view, the tests that a carbon credit must meet prior to being created are often considerably more rigorous than reported internal emissions reductions – see Myth #4 below.

To dispel this myth we think that the industry needs to explain the process of generating an 'emissions reduction' or carbon credit more clearly and to use consistent terminology – the generic noun used should be emission reduction or carbon credit – with 'offset' used as a verb – 'I offset my emissions.'

Myth #2: You can't trust offsets – they're not real

With the emergence of credible and independent standards and registries such as the Voluntary Carbon Standard (VCS) and Gold Standard, we hope that this particular myth is on its way out. However, we should recognize that the regulated carbon market and in particular the CDM also faces this challenge. In November 2007, WWF published the results of a report it had commissioned into the effectiveness of the CDM, and the main conclusion was that '20 per cent of the CERs issued ($\sim$34MtCO$_2$) may have happened without CDM financing'. While the media picked up this headline, the implication of this conclusion is that 80 per cent of the reductions ($\sim$140MtCO$_2$) *did* result from the existence of the CDM. Elsewhere in WWF's report – not reported to the same extent in the media – there was a strong endorsement from WWF: 'If the problems identified here are properly addressed, the CDM will continue to be an important instrument in the fight against climate change.'

To dispel this myth, the industry needs proactively to communicate the real benefits of project-based carbon finance and to build on the institutions and processes that have been developed in the regulated market, such as the Executive Board and the process for developing new methodologies. We should recognize that one negative story about a poor quality project undermines the good work and real reductions achieved by ten high quality, probably unreported projects.

Myth #3: Companies must choose between offsetting and reductions

There exists the view that if a company is offsetting part of its emissions, it is making no other efforts to reduce its climate impact, and that it has simply paid its way out of the problem (see Myth #5 below). In our experience this is rarely, if ever, the case. Indeed, companies that are rapidly growing often set 'relative' reduction targets that are linked to numbers of employees or turnover, meaning that if business growth is greater than the reduction target, then an alleged internal 'reduction' will result in an absolute *increase* in emissions. Offsetting, however, provides a way to benchmark the costs of internal emissions reductions against an external figure and a 'safety valve' to achieve that portion of a true and absolute reduction target that cannot be met cost-effectively within the boundary of the business itself.

Our hypothesis is that companies using offsetting as part of their carbon management strategy achieve greater internal reductions and greater net reductions than those that don't. Companies will need to demonstrate that offsetting is just one part of a broader carbon management programme and that it provides the most economically rational way to achieve the necessary scaleable targets.

Myth #4: Internal emissions reductions are more credible than offsets

Accounting systems for carbon credits have become increasingly sophisticated. Project proponents must now demonstrate that they have considered a number of baseline scenarios; the impacts of the project outside the project boundaries have to be properly accounted for (leakage); an appropriate monitoring plan has to be developed and followed (exactly); and the outputs must be independently verified in order for credits to be issued. In addition, project documentation is made public and open to third party challenge.

Contrast this with much reporting of internal emissions reductions, which is subject to far fewer checks and balances. A company that outsources manufacturing to China to save costs, for example, may close down a UK factory in the process – resulting in lower reported emissions for the company but similar (or potentially higher due to increased transport) total emissions for the delivery of products to consumers.

In short, carbon market players, while not being complacent, should be proud of the level of transparency surrounding the issuance of high quality carbon credits, and should not shy away from challenging reported internal emissions reductions that don't meet similar accounting standards.

Myth #5: Offsetting is like selling indulgences – it doesn't drive behavioural change

This is linked to Myth #3 – the fallacy that companies offsetting emissions are not generally driven to reduce emissions internally. There are two sound business reasons for not following this approach. The first is that by offsetting, businesses are voluntarily taking on an additional cost, and there is therefore an economic incentive to reduce a cost that was previously invisible. The second reason is that the media and other stakeholders are highly sceptical about environmental claims, and if they are not seen to have substance, the company may face negative publicity as a result. While it would be false to claim that every company that offsets has an equally good carbon management programme, it is equally false to assume that without the 'easy way out' of offsetting these companies would all have deep internal reductions programmes in place.

To dispel this myth, companies with offset programmes should communicate all aspects of their carbon management activities and demonstrate with actual examples how offsetting has led to changes in behaviour for them or their customers.

Myth #6: There is not enough 'capacity' for all emissions to be offset

This is the only myth that has an element of truth to it – but again it results from a misunderstanding of what offsetting does. Offsetting is about financing new technologies that reduce emissions; if there is no capacity left to create projects that reduce emissions, it means that emissions are already at zero and we will have achieved our goal of a zero-carbon world!

Moving forward

To summarize, the science around global warming isn't going to reverse, and it seems impossible to accelerate international negotiations, so the best way to break the logjam is to massively scale-up voluntary action. The key catalysts needed are:

- Strong government endorsement of high quality voluntary carbon instruments as complementary to mandatory emissions caps and carbon taxes.
- Focus on a small number of high quality standards and demonstrate that these are as good if not better than current CDM standards.
- Tangible, large-scale examples of how voluntary offsetting activities have resulted in better decision-making and real reductions.
- Finding ways to enable high quality, additional 'domestic' projects in Kyoto Annexe 1 countries. Our experience is that there is strong demand from business and consumers to contribute to emissions reductions close to home.
- For service providers to the voluntary market to commit to levels of transparency and public reporting of their activities to bring confidence to the sector and to work towards developing a common understanding of the term 'carbon neutral'.

Unless the voluntary market is thinking about how to deliver reductions in excess of 1 gigatonne by the middle of the next decade, it will be a sideshow that makes no material contribution. The voluntary carbon market has grown up a lot over the last couple of years – the challenge is now for it to make a real impact on the problem it has set itself up to solve.

A credit originator's perspective on the voluntary carbon markets: Encouraging quality in the markets

Mark C. Trexler
EcoSecurities

Environmental commodity markets are emerging as a preferred mechanism for addressing increasingly complicated environmental objectives, from biodiversity loss to climate change. As we develop these new markets, standards that hold environmental commodities to a minimum level of quality are increasingly seen as critical to the integrity of the voluntary carbon markets.

In the voluntary carbon markets, additionality is the key to ensuring market credibility. However, as the voluntary markets have rapidly expanded in recent years, with a diverse and growing group of verified emission reduction (VER) providers, a common test for project additionality has been elusive. As a result, the environmental integrity of VERs is far from assured in today's market. Organizations making a good-faith effort to mitigate their CO_2 footprint risk facing charges of greenwashing by observers or reporters sceptical of the environmental integrity of VERs. The 2007 Academy Awards purchased VERs in order to declare their presenters carbon neutral, but ran into criticism when these credits turned out to fail a basic additionality test (Elgin, 2007). Today's lack of quality control for VERs is a serious challenge to achieving the long-term potential of the voluntary carbon markets.

Today, a number of organizations are proposing standards for use in the voluntary carbon markets. This article reviews the challenges facing such standards, and proposes an alternative approach to informing the markets about offset quality. We conclude that a sophisticated system for scoring offset quality, including additionality, can provide market participants with a great deal more information than is available through a basic standard.

Challenges facing standards

Offset quality is determined by a number of variables, but the most important single issue, whether in voluntary or mandatory markets, is the additionality of the project and associated emissions reductions. Any voluntary carbon standard, no matter how well intentioned, faces the challenge of seeking to limit the prevalence of so-called 'false positives' in the offset pool, and seeking to identify which projects' emissions reductions are ultimately attributable to the existence of the voluntary carbon market. The challenge in cracking down on 'false positives' is to not push too many 'real' reductions out of the offset pool as 'false negatives'. As in any statistical hypothesis testing, you can't minimize for both false negatives and false positives simultaneously (Trexler et al, 2006).

In reality, assessing the additionality of a given GHG mitigation project is not as simple as the 'thumbs-up' or 'thumbs-down' approach that a basic 'in or out' standard implies. There is a quality continuum when it comes to carbon offsets, from clearly additional projects and reductions to clearly non-additional projects and reductions. The use of a standard usually does not recognize the existence of this continuum. Instead, a project that barely fails the standard is labelled as a bad project, whereas a project that barely passes the standard is considered a good project. The two projects might be almost identical. The problem arises in that, once a project has passed or failed the standard, it is impossible for the market to differentiate where the reductions actually fall on the quality continuum. Are they at the lower end of the continuum, but still above the minimum threshold set by the standard, or at the higher end where we would like the market to go? Even if two projects meet a certain standard's minimum quality requirements, one may be of much higher quality than the other. A standard does nothing to differentiate these projects in the eyes of consumers, and fails to deliver a lot of the information that could help consumers make better decisions.

In addition, a single standard also has difficulty in responding to the multiple motivations and preferences different participants in the market may have. Some participants may place more weight on local projects or the ancillary benefits of projects. For others, cost-effective reductions will be more important. It is virtually impossible for a single standard to inform consumers of a project's performance against the possible range of attributes.

Benefits of a project scoring system

The alternative to a single-threshold voluntary market standard is the development of a project scoring system. A scoring system could be used to rank projects along a continuum on the basis of multiple quality variables. A project score of 300 out of 1000 would suggest fundamental uncertainty with regard to the project's additionality and overall quality. A project score of 600 out of 1000 would suggest a much more robust project, but not necessarily a top-tier project. A score of 900 out of 1000 would suggest not only a high degree of confidence in the project's additionality, but advanced performance in areas like co-benefits as well.

Such a scoring tool would have three primary impacts:

1   It would provide purchasers with a great deal of information about a project's actual performance, and where it sits on the quality continuum.
2   It would encourage the market to strive for higher quality. All things being equal, purchasers will seek out the highest scoring offsets that they can.
3   It would allow for designing a portfolio of reductions that are of comparable quality. Retail offset providers, for example, might choose not to add

anything to their portfolio that scores below 750, increasing consumers' confidence in their offsets.

All of these impacts represent major advantages over a simple threshold standard. Figure 4.2 illustrates how the quality continuum can vary across sectors. The great majority of potential projects involving permanent reforestation along riparian zones, for example, are likely to score highly on additionality and co-benefits. It's also relatively easy to demonstrate the additionality of many small-scale coal mine recovery projects. A much smaller fraction of energy efficiency projects, however, can demonstrate clear additionality. This is not to say that energy efficiency projects can't be additional; they obviously can. However, there are so many energy efficiency projects underway for so many reasons already that it's much harder to differentiate clearly additional projects.

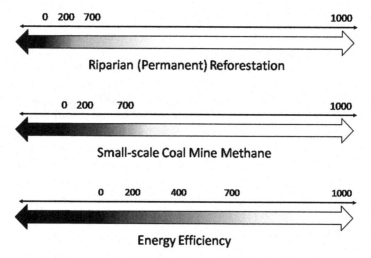

Figure 4.2 *Project additionality across the continuum in riparian reforestation, small-scale coal mine methane, and energy efficiency projects*

Conclusion

Offset quality is key to achieving the climate change mitigation benefits of the voluntary carbon market. That said, the challenge of developing and implementing quality standards for voluntary carbon markets goes beyond overcoming political hurdles and into dealing with the realities of carbon offsets. Proposed voluntary carbon market standards can create a floor for offset quality, but they will have a great deal of difficulty going further than that. A rating system allows projects of varying degrees of additionality and quality to be compared side by side, thus providing buyers in the marketplace greater knowledge, choice and security. This should lead not only to more confidence in the market, but also to the creation of incentives for the market to push towards higher quality offsets.

An investor's perspective on the voluntary carbon markets:
From marginal to mainstream

David Brand and Marisa Meizlish
New Forests

Long before there was a Kyoto Protocol or an EU ETS, carbon transactions were occurring. The earliest deals (related to forest conservation and reforestation) began in the late 1980s. Through the 1990s the retail and voluntary markets grew slowly, but certain key developments began to emerge. Companies whose entire business focused on carbon markets were born, including Ecosecurities, Future Forests (now The CarbonNeutral Company), Natsource, CantorCO2e and Evolution Markets. The concept of green power, linked with renewable energy and tree planting programmes as offset sources for automobile and air travel emissions, began to develop.

While the overall carbon market shuddered for two or three years after the withdrawal of the US from the Kyoto Protocol, the retail and voluntary markets continued to diversify. The CCX was established in 2003 as the first voluntary carbon credit market. Retail carbon companies proliferated, and there are now more than 90 worldwide. On the demand side, the concept of businesses offsetting some or all of their emissions has become widely adopted, and carbon investment funds are allocating larger portions of their portfolios to voluntary offsets. Investment spending and buyer confidence is growing, in part because of access to more robust market analysis and information.

At the tipping point

Organizations ranging in size and character – from small NGOs to financial companies to major multinational corporations – are determining that climate change is an important issue to their customers and stakeholders. The response has been to take action by measuring and reducing the GHG emissions associated with their business activities or products. An important development in just the past one to two years is the consideration of supply chain impacts, with businesses looking beyond their own offices or operations to consider emissions related to transportation, suppliers and distributors. While any consideration of these issues may have been seen as more of a marketing gimmick five years ago, its recent embrace by major mainstream businesses has pushed the voluntary carbon markets to a tipping point.

The focus is shifting from the innovators to the laggards, and the question is being asked, 'Why haven't you offset your emissions?' Companies that have a corporate social responsibility policy or have made statements supporting action on climate change are moving from vague emission reduction commitments to quantifiable reduction targets and how offsets can help achieve them. Programmes such as the US EPA's Climate Leaders publicize the emission reduction commitments of companies and work to develop transparent method-ologies to measure, monitor and reduce emissions over time. These companies, and others like them around the world, are taking bold steps ahead of legislation, voluntarily committing to emission reductions of a few percentage points to more than 30 per cent over the next five to ten years.

A weird and wonderful world

Voluntary and retail carbon offset products include a host of offset types origi-nating from tree planting, forest conservation, industrial gas destruction, energy efficiency programmes, renewable energy credits, changes in animal husbandry or waste management, changes in vehicle fleets and many others. The retail and voluntary markets are certainly not 'commoditized' at this point, but with the entry into the markets of large and reputable buyers, the writing is on the wall for poorly defined or managed offset programmes. Buyers now want standardized offsets with real evidence of additionality and truly independent verification of the reductions. There is also a growing demand for projects that have other social and environmental benefits, such as local employment or biodiversity protection. Buyers do not necessarily want to buy Kyoto units or other regulated carbon products, largely because they generally are more expensive. Carbon offset project developers, particularly those developing small projects or project types not well accepted under Kyoto (e.g. forest conservation and reforestation), also find the lower transaction costs and lack of bureaucratic accreditation processes make the route to market easier in the voluntary markets.

The markets are quickly coalescing around a suite of standards that are set-ting the bar for high quality voluntary offsets. In particular, the VCS, released in 2007, is garnering significant buyer preference and higher prices. It is becoming the de facto market expectation, and project developers are building projects to the requirements of this standard. The Climate, Community & Biodiversity Alliance (CCBA) Standard is also widely recognized and is often used in con-junction with the VCS. While the VCS provides confidence around such funda-mental elements as the accounting methodology, permanence and leakage, the CCBA standard signals additional biodiversity and social benefits associated with projects. A double certification across these standards, specifically for land-based projects such as forest conservation or reforestation, will be highly attractive to the marketplace.

Forest-based offsets

Forestry credits have been a mainstay in the voluntary and retail carbon market from the very earliest deals by AES Corporation and the FACE foundation to protect rainforests in the late 1980s and early 1990s. However, the negotiations concerning the Kyoto Protocol forestry rules were protracted and strongly influ-enced by a group of environmental NGOs who sought to minimize the role of forestry in market-based mechanisms. The legacy of this has been a minimal role for forestry under the Kyoto Protocol and its international mechanisms, particularly related to forest conservation, which was unilaterally determined to be an ineligible activity. Nevertheless, several carbon markets are successfully integrating forestry credits, including the NSW Greenhouse Gas Abatement Scheme, the CCAR-inspired market and the CCX.

Forestry credits are very attractive in the retail and voluntary markets. One energy company polled its customers on the kinds of offsets they would prefer if the company were to offer a green energy product. Compared against industrial gas destruction, relining pipelines, improving energy efficiency in office buildings and factories and capturing methane from coal mines, forestry was far and away the preferred source of offsets. Companies indicate that the concept of using trees and forests for offsets makes sense to consumers, while trying to explain methane destruction or sulphur hexafluoride destruction is confusing and simply does not resonate. As one company executive explained, 'We have been using trees as the imagery of environmental conservation forever, and trying to re-educate consumers to understand methane flaring is too hard.'

However, despite this demand, many of the current initiatives to standardize offsets are falling into a 'Kyoto mindset' on forestry. There are real concerns about permanence and measurement, and these issues are often used to argue that forestry offsets are simply too hard to regulate effectively.

For example, a carbon credit from a forestry project may require an ability to retain carbon stock in forests for 100 years or more. This kind of intergenerational obligation is as compelling as it is daunting. New and innovative approaches are needed to address this, including specialized carbon-pooling vehicles, reinsurance approaches and risk management systems. The VCS has offered the market the most innovative option to date, using a pooled buffer stock in which projects reduce the amount of saleable carbon based on a permanence risk assessment. The pooled buffer stock across all forestry projects hedges against the potential loss of carbon over time in any one project.

Efforts to exclude forestry projects originally led to investors shying away from land-based offsets, reducing access to funding and resources dedicated to establishing permanence protocols and measurement standards – the very issues that have been used to keep forestry credits on the sidelines. Recently, forestry credits have been on a comeback, bolstered in part by the increasing recognition that carbon finance could have a role to play in addressing tropical rainforest deforestation and biodiversity loss.

The UNFCCC Conference of the Parties (COP) meeting in Montreal in 2005 (COP11) responded positively to a proposal sponsored by Papua New Guinea and Costa Rica to reopen the discussion on how to accredit avoided deforestation. At COP13 in Bali in 2007, avoided deforestation – now under the name Reduced Emissions from Deforestation and Degradation (REDD) – was firmly a central point of debate at the highest levels. The Bali Roadmap agreed to at COP13 set the stage for REDD to be considered in a post-2012 Kyoto framework with the decision to be made by COP15 in Copenhagen in 2009. These decisions have resulted in a flurry of investment activity in REDD projects with two large project announcements in 2008 – Flora & Fauna

International's work in Aceh, Indonesia, and New Forests' project in Papua, Indonesia. These and other investors have an eye towards initial transactions in the voluntary markets, scaling up to opportunities in Kyoto and other regulatory markets.

Towards the future

It appears clear that the voluntary carbon markets are growing rapidly and moving to a new level of standardization and legitimacy. If we reach the tipping point where business begins to move in a substantial way to integrate carbon offsets into its internal management objectives and product offerings, the markets could increase by orders of magnitude.

Ecosystems, particularly forested ecosystems, provide a natural infrastructure for the planet, regulating the atmosphere, hydrological cycles and much of the biodiversity of life on earth. Forests continue to be lost and degraded, and areas needing re-vegetation or reforestation struggle to attract investment. Without price signals for ecosystem services, including carbon sequestration, we are entrenching the status quo of existing economic signals and dooming a significant proportion of our remaining tropical forests to conversion to non-forest land uses. Once converted, these forests are unlikely to return.

An investor's perspective: The challenges ahead for scaling the voluntary carbon markets

Alexander Rau
Climate Wedge Ltd

Carbon markets and emissions trading have emerged over the past few years as two of the most promising response options to the growing problem of climate change. While most attention has been focused on the EU ETS and the CDM/JI project markets under the Kyoto Protocol, voluntary carbon markets have been experiencing rapid growth as well. Proactive corporations are beginning to unlock hidden shareholder value by using project-based emissions reductions as a tool complementing internal measures to achieve self-imposed carbon neutrality commitments and prepare for emerging regulatory constraints, or in offering carbon offset products and services in sectors with few short-term technology solutions.

But as with any nascent market there are a number of critical issues as to how the voluntary carbon markets will develop over the next few years. These will largely determine what role this market will play in the overall effort to mitigate the climate problem. With a continuation of current market practices one might expect modest growth from present volumes.

At this level the voluntary carbon markets will be an 'affectionate' attempt at reducing emissions and would play an important role in educating the public about climate change, but they will not have a meaningful impact on the climate problem.

Conservative estimates from the scientific community suggest that reductions in excess of 500 billion tons of CO_2e are necessary between now and the middle of the century simply to avoid a doubling of the pre-industrial concentration of carbon in the atmosphere. A well-scaled voluntary carbon market could drive reductions in the order of hundreds of millions of tons per year, and thus can have a more meaningful impact on shifting the emissions trajectory. The theoretical potential for volumes exceeding this scale exists because of the ability of voluntary markets to target sectors that are beyond the reach of efficient regulation, such as with mobile or diffuse sources in the transportation or building sectors. Even regulated sectors typically face incremental caps or reduction targets, leaving the majority of emissions unabated. Furthermore, the consumer-facing nature of many voluntary initiatives allows for steady growth subject more to marketing dynamics and intrinsic demand than political dynamics and the volatility of artificial demand. But in order for the voluntary market to scale to such a meaningful size there are a number of challenges that must be addressed.

Uniform quality standard

First is the need for a consistent set of internationally accepted standards determining which projects create reductions that are truly 'real, quantifiable and permanent', and the procedures by which these reductions are calculated, monitored and verified. Recent and persistent critical press coverage of the voluntary markets only highlights the urgency for agreement on best-practice quality standards for the markets. A number of initiatives have arisen in the last two years, most notably the VCS, which was launched for active trading in 2006 and has subsequently undergone numerous stakeholder-driven revisions. Much of the strength of the VCS lies in its adoption of the experience and intelligence built up over several years in the international project markets – namely, a large set of project-specific methodologies that have been road tested with billions of dollars of capital across hundreds of projects, and a group of experienced verifiers. It remains to be seen, however, whether the VCS and other standards initiatives such as the Gold Standard can promote credibility and harmonization in the voluntary markets without imposing an excessive and arbitrary bureaucracy on the project approval process.

Standardized reduction

In order to scale appreciably, the voluntary markets also need to move towards a standardized reduction unit. The fungible nature of the underlying tradable instrument is a key factor contributing to the liquidity of most large financial markets. The current emphasis on linking voluntary carbon credits to particular high-visibility projects may have transitional communication benefits but is not a model that can scale to drive large volumes of emissions reductions or ensure a reliable supply of carbon for voluntary initiatives at realistic costs.

Instead, the burden of quality should rest on the standards as discussed above, in which case the reductions verified to have met the standard can effectively be treated as fungible. This was one of the original objectives in the launching of the first version of the VCS, namely to create confidence behind a 'voluntary carbon unit' or VCU as a market instrument itself. Although the market is not yet comfortable with fungibility for voluntary carbon instruments, this would be a critical development for managing delivery provisions in forward contracts and thus facilitating investment into future voluntary projects, as opposed to the current practice of simply transacting existing reduction units.

Robust market infrastructure

Recognizing that carbon credits from GHG abatement projects should be treated as financial assets, the voluntary markets must develop comparable infrastructure to that which exists in other asset classes but tailored to the specific attributes of carbon. The principle components are a custodial registry and retirement platform. Procedures must also be in place to ensure that verified reductions are not double counted, counterparty and settlement risks can be effectively managed and the retirement of credits can be transparently reported. A number of registry platforms are emerging – including a custodial registry service launched in 2006 by the Bank of New York and which was recently accredited as an official registry for the VCS Version 2 – that address these concerns and should give confidence to investors and corporate end-users alike that voluntary carbon assets can be managed in the same reliable manner as are other financial instruments.

Return on investment

Finally, voluntary carbon must still prove itself to be a sufficiently attractive investment opportunity in its own right in order to mobilize private capital to finance high quality GHG abatement projects in situations where compliance instruments cannot be created. Its track record to date has been mixed. The offset model must also be economically attractive to motivate corporate providers of carbon-intensive products and services to offer transitional offset solutions where there are no short-term technological options or regulatory requirements. Ultimately these corporations are providing customers with an 'environmental service', the revenues from which will spur them to seek innovative ways to develop and market low carbon/offset products and services.

Thus far, the short life of the voluntary market has seen reasonable growth despite modest progress on each of the above issues. Going forward, however, standardization, market infrastructure and return on investment will continue to be the dominant considerations, alongside any potential interactions with emerging regulatory regimes. Serious and coordinated efforts to address these issues will help lay the appropriate conditions for the voluntary carbon market to scale meaningfully. The magnitude of the challenge of stabilizing the atmospheric concentrations of carbon at manageable levels of risk makes it clear that all of the viable response options must be adopted, whether regulatory or voluntary, cap-and-trade or technology-based approaches. A large and robust voluntary market for project-based emissions has a significant transitional role to play in increasing the flow of funds towards low carbon technologies and shifting the global emissions trajectory.

A buyer's perspective on the voluntary carbon markets: Lessons learned in the early days of carbon neutrality

Erin Meezan
Interface, Inc

Carbon neutrality was still a fringe concept in 2003, when Interface, the largest modular carpet manufacturer in the world, launched Cool Carpet™ – one of the first climate neutral products in the world and the first third party-verified, climate neutral product to receive the Climate Cool™ certification in the US.

Since then, consumers have purchased 52 million square yards of climate-neutral carpet, leading to the purchase and retirement of close to 1 million tons of CO_2.

In 2007, Interface made climate neutrality a standard attribute of most of its products sold globally – cementing its status as a significant purchaser in the voluntary carbon market with an informed perspective on the market's impact to date, as well as the challenges and opportunities facing it in the future.

Early learning

When we first started talking to sellers of offsets in 2003, a hodgepodge of offsets were being sold under very different standards, with the due diligence burden falling mostly on buyers and the resulting *quality* of offsets being hit-or-miss.

This began to improve in 2005 and really came together in 2007, when the launch of new standards and growing stakeholder interest forced greater transparency in the marketplace.

Now, a few standards have clearly won more trust than others – primarily the VCS and the Gold Standard for VERs. Prices still vary from one standard to another, but the market is getting closer to consistent pricing of offsets. More importantly, the level of transparency in the market has improved, so buyers can get a sense of the prices they should pay. Further, there is an ability to understand the link between quality and higher price that wasn't there in the past.

One positive surprise has been the dramatic increase in the desire of our stakeholders – including internal employees and customers – to understand how we source offsets, where they are applied in our business and how credible they are.

What we did right and what we would change

What we did right

Interface has always had a strong commitment to sustainability, and this culture drove us to focus on developing a highly credible carbon neutral product programme. For us, this meant a very diligent approach to not only calculating our product footprint, but making sure we were using credible offsets. The only way in the early days to ensure we were buying credible offsets was to immerse ourselves in the voluntary carbon market.

We attended meetings and events on the voluntary market, and were often the only corporate buyer there. We also tried to learn by talking to project developers, brokers and NGOs who were working in the market.

We were also asked to serve on committees and councils, and to give guidance to other buyers. I was surprised be invited onto the Steering Committee for the creation of the VCS and to advise on the Center for Resource Solution's Green-e GHG Standard. Offering our perspective and concerns ultimately helped us shape future standards, albeit in tiny ways, with buyers in mind.

As our knowledge grew, we started to know exactly what type of offset we wanted. We started to avoid certain project types – such as forestry projects – because of credibility, location or monitoring and verification issues.

Over time, we developed a set of internal criteria against which to measure potential purchases of offsets. These criteria include not only credibility issues like whether the offsets are real, permanent, verifiable and additional (which are requirements now basic to most standards), but also additional social benefits and a price range that we will not exceed. These criteria now help us streamline our process in screening offset purchases.

After a few years as a buyer, we realized we needed a strategy for adapting to price increases in the future. We also saw the voluntary market start to put a recognizable premium on exactly the kinds of offsets that had special relevance for us: those with benefits beyond carbon reduction or avoidance – credits sometimes referred to as 'gourmet' or charismatic carbon offsets. These are offsets from projects that have attributable local economic benefits, employ local populations, and have social or community benefits or are experimenting with exciting technologies and 'firsts'.

As a first step towards controlling pricing, we moved away from buying all of our offsets from these charismatic projects and towards a portfolio of offsets that included some charismatic offsets along with other offsets that met minimum credibility standards but were without these additional benefits. A side benefit that emerged from having a diverse portfolio of projects was the marketing benefit of multiple project stories to tell. And, as a global business, the portfolio approach allows us more flexibility to source offsets from a range of locations around the world. This also satisfies our internal stakeholders, who want to see offsets from projects in their part of the world.

Over the past five years, we also identified processes that companies might follow to make sure they are purchasing credible offsets. A great first step for us was launching a Request for Proposals (RFP) process, which helped to both identify who the sellers were and get a broad range of proposals and prices.

At first, we relied on sellers to provide the contracts when we purchased off-sets. The agreements were typically quite short, and very few of them adequately protected the full interests of buyers. They often did not include confidentiality provisions, and many did not address the unique risks involved in buying offsets and the potential damages to a buyer if the obligations were not fulfilled. In response to this, we retained outside counsel to draft an agreement that we now use for all carbon offset purchases. Today, there are templates available for buyers, and both the International Emissions Trading Association (IETA) and the American Bar Association have standard documents.

What we would do differently

When we first launched the Cool Carpet™ programme, we didn't have a clear sense of exactly what constituted a credible offset. We knew that it needed to be real, permanent, verifiable and additional, but in 2003 we weren't exactly sure how we could determine additionality. We ended up using an organization called the Climate Neutral Network, newly launched in the US to help companies develop climate neutral products and services. We presented our potential Cool Carpet™ offsets to this organization and its environmental advisory board, and essentially asked them to determine the additionality and appropriateness of the offsets. By today's standards, the process lacked rigour and documentation, but that is often the case with early movers and innovators. Nonetheless, it left us with a strong sense that we were using credible offsets.

With the evolution of standards like the Gold Standard for VERs and the VCS, which are essentially verification programmes with additionality tests inherent in them, we can simply purchase offsets already verified to these standards or to the CDM standard.

In retrospect, a second weakness of our programme and offset purchasing in the early days was the lack of retirement mechanisms. Lacking any registries, we simply purchased offsets and made sure we never used them again. Only one seller we worked with had partnered with a non-profit to actually retire tons by giving them to this non-profit who certified they were never used again. Perhaps, in retrospect, we should have developed some sort of similar arrangement for retirement. Although we can show exactly where our offsets were applied and that they were never re-used, it exists only in our internal documentation.

The way we purchased our offsets in the beginning could also have been done better. The offset purchases we made were typically one-year agreements for small volumes (10,000–20,000 tons). In retrospect, we regret not setting up longer-term contracts given the ensuing rise in prices and current lack of availability of carbon offsets from some of our early projects. Not only did we not sign multi-year purchase agreements, but we didn't even think to ask for options on future tons, whether at fixed or negotiable prices.

Lastly, we significantly under-marketed our carbon neutral product programme – in large part because we were not sure how to communicate it clearly to customers. While we are generally acknowledged as being the first in our industry and one of the first in the world to offer a carbon neutral product, we did not enjoy great recognition of the effort outside of our industry and the carbon neutral community. This is improving as our customers and stakeholders come to understand what carbon neutral means, and as we learn to highlight Cool Carpet™ as a differentiator in our marketing.

Current challenges with engaging in the market: Update

Over the past year and a half, the voluntary carbon markets have made significant progress towards a common standard and supporting framework, but the markets still lack universal agreement in key areas.

What is still holding the markets back here? One factor is the time that it takes to launch and then gain support for one standard. The VCS was launched after numerous delays, then had challenges to overcome in fully launching – including the development of protocols and its registry. While there has been significant movement towards the VCS as this one unifying standard, we're not there yet.

A second factor is that others are still developing their own standards. These multiple standards only create more confusion.

At the same time, it is still difficult to find offsets that meet the Gold and Voluntary Carbon Standards. When we ask sellers for tons meeting these standards, we're constantly told that projects are 'in the process', but few have tons that are ready to deliver.

Transparency has still not evolved to a satisfactory point, either, particularly for new entrants to the markets. What passes for market data is often anecdotal and amassed through voluntary surveys. Much more transparency is needed to help us all have a better understanding of where the markets and prices are heading in three to five years.

Finally, the lack of a centralized registry system still makes retirement and monitoring a challenge for buyers and sellers. Currently, Interface is retiring its offsets in a range of different registries, with the decision on those highly dependent on the region of projects.

Company-specific challenges and how Interface is navigating them

Interface, as a large corporate buyer with a voluntary programme, has its own unique challenges. Keeping the prices we pay for offsets stable and predictable, as we expand the programme, is critical. As our programme grows and we are acknowledged for our leadership in carbon neutrality, we face an increasing need to provide greater details on the programme itself, footprint calculations and offset purchases.

Because one of the biggest challenges for us is price stability, we are purchasing in larger volumes and seeking and signing longer-term purchase commitments. We are also looking beyond just the purchase of offsets and adding into our agreements options on certain yet-to-be-identified offsets at fixed prices.

To manage risks to the credibility of our programme or our carbon offset deals, we are constantly revising our standard carbon offset purchase agreements. These ever-improving transactional documents now include standard confidentiality clauses, as well as broader protections like liquidated damages clauses that would protect Interface in the event of any unique harm to our programme from a deal not being completed.

Meeting the desires of stakeholders for greater detail on our carbon offsets will simply require greater transparency from us, which means our demanding more details from sellers. Evolving standards like the VCS will help, but in the interim we are simply trying to disclose as much information as possible to stakeholders by identifying projects on our websites and providing more specific details on the processes. This means we are asking sellers up front what level of disclosure they can provide on projects, and using this as an assessment of whether or not to buy the offsets.

Many of these solutions are interim ones, and we are actively exploring what our response should be in the future. We are also exploring several new initiatives including banding with other like-minded companies to purchase offsets together, forming a partnership with sellers who develop their own projects to have a say in what types of projects are developed, and possibly securing access to a unique pool of offsets, or even developing our own projects with a supplier.

Future hopes: What still needs to be done

It seems we are past the wave of scepticism about the legitimacy of carbon offsets and are moving into an environment where offsets are more accepted, but more transparency will be required. Project-based transparency will be required from a broader range of buyers and their stakeholders. This is greatly needed to both facilitate more confidence in transactions and to satisfy new market entrants and stakeholders. The new voluntary market entrants, both buyers and sellers, need plenty of education, but their choices are easier nowadays. Finally, we need more ways for corporations to have long-term investment in and support of projects that really make a difference to the planet. Whether this is achieved through their collaboration in buying pools, or by working with project developers to define projects that are of best fit, remains to be determined.

A bank's perspective on the voluntary carbon markets: From risk to opportunity

Lorna Slade
HSBC

In 2005, HSBC became the world's first major bank – and FTSE 100 company – to achieve carbon neutrality. The decision to become carbon neutral took HSBC into uncharted territory, so the company began by examining the carbon footprint of its operations around the world. The bank then consulted external experts, built in-house capability and established a carbon management task-force with members drawn from all corners of the organization. The result was a multidisciplinary committee to advise on the policy and process of becoming carbon neutral. This ensured commitment from all business areas.

Today, the bank continually assesses its carbon footprint, reduces energy consumption where possible and offsets any remaining CO_2 emissions. Why has HSBC chosen to lead on the issue of climate change when it is not subject to any climate change legislation? Francis Sullivan, HSBC's Adviser on the Environment, explains:

> *HSBC believes that climate change is the greatest single environmental, social and economic challenge facing the business community this century. Being carbon neutral reflects our desire to confront this challenge in a proactive and productive way.*

Compared to a major manufacturer or energy company, HSBC is not a significant emitter of CO_2, but as a global organization employing 330,000 people in 10,000 offices across 83 countries, Sullivan says, 'achieving carbon neutrality is not something that just happens overnight. Going carbon neutral requires careful planning and thorough execution, just like any other major business endeavour.'

Carbon management plan

There are four key steps the bank uses to achieve its carbon neutrality:

1 *Measure.* HSBC measures the energy usage in its buildings and tracks employee business travel to calculate its carbon footprint. Almost all of HSBC's employees work in branches or offices where energy use and the resulting carbon footprint are measured and reported publicly.

2 *Reduce.* The bank reduces its carbon footprint where possible. In addition to setting challenging energy and CO_2 reduction targets, the bank has implemented a range of energy-saving office projects, such as the installation of low-energy lighting, software to power down computers that are not in use,

and improved building insulation. HSBC has also installed state-of-the-art video-conferencing technology to reduce the need for business travel.

3   *Purchase green.* HSBC buys green electricity in a number of countries around the world, including the UK and the US, to help decarbonize the electricity it uses.

4   *Offset.* HSBC voluntarily offsets its remaining emissions. The bank purchases emission reductions from a range of projects around the world including renewable energy and energy efficiency projects.

HSBC purchases VERs from projects approved and registered (but not yet certified) by the CDM Executive Board and may purchase offsets through a number of offset providers or brokers, as well as from project owners and the bank's own clients.

Extensive due diligence is undertaken on all potential offset projects. In addition, all offsets are validated and verified to recognized market standards by an independent third party.

HSBC seeks to procure emissions reductions that meet the following criteria:

• Additionality – that is, the underlying project would not have occurred in the absence of carbon finance.
• The underlying project should support the transition to a low carbon economy.
• The underlying project should have clearly defined, long-term sustainable development benefits.

The bank seeks to develop a portfolio that supports a wide variety of technologies from projects all around the world. Information about these projects is made publicly available on the HSBC website (www.hsbc.com).

Since first becoming carbon neutral in 2005, HSBC has launched the Global Environmental Efficiency Programme, a US$90 million programme over five years to reduce its environmental impact through the introduction of renewable energy technologies, water and waste reduction initiatives and employee engagement programmes. The programme enables HSBC offices to showcase environmental innovation and share best practices that help achieve the bank's reduction targets for energy and CO_2.

HSBC's efforts have not gone without notice. The bank has received environmental accolades for new buildings constructed in Mexico City, Chicago, New York, Hyderabad and London. Earlier this year, the bank installed 617 square metres of photovoltaic panels on the roof of its HQ in Canary Wharf, London, reflecting its continuous drive to improve environmental efficiency and showcase innovation.

'[HSBC's] ongoing commitment to carbon neutrality is part of a holistic strategy,' says Jon Williams, former Head of Group Sustainable Development at HSBC. 'This includes not only the carbon footprint of [the company's] property portfolio and purchasing decisions, but also [its] core business activities of lending and investing.'

Climate change as a strategic issue

So what is the thinking behind making climate change such an important issue?

Intrinsic to this is an understanding that the impacts of climate change will affect HSBC's global operations as well as its employees, shareholders, business partners and ultimately, the products and services it offers customers.

'The evidence is overwhelming and compelling for a financial institution like ours. Ultimately the impacts of climate change affect the very basis upon which we currently do business,' says Williams.

A key motivation behind HSBC's decision to become carbon neutral was a need to understand the implications and impacts that an increasingly carbon-constrained economy will have for the bank and its clients. The costs of carbon are expected to increase as a result of regulation and carbon taxes, and the bank firmly believes that financial institutions should and will play an important role in the shift to a low carbon economy. As a result, the bank has spearheaded a number of initiatives to help clients and customers seeking low carbon alternatives.

Commitment to climate change is driven at the most senior level. In 2007, Lord Nicholas Stern was appointed to advise HSBC on economic development and climate change and since then has engaged in international debate on climate change at Bali and at the World Economic Forum in Davos.

HSBC has an established team that focuses on corporate sustainability at the Group level to lead the bank's strategy in this area. In addition to ensuring that the bank continues to reduce its impact on the environment and remain carbon neutral, the team is responsible for expanding the bank's capability in financing renewable energy projects, managing the environmental and social risks of its lending activity and maximizing the related opportunities presented to the bank and its clients.

'Over the next five years HSBC will make responding to climate change central to our business operations and to the way in which we work with our clients across the world,' says Group Chairman Stephen Green. The Corporate Sustainability team is also responsible for launching a five-year, £50 million programme called The HSBC Climate Partnership, in conjunction with four leading environmental charities – WWF, The Smithsonian Tropical Research Institute, The Climate Group and Earthwatch Institute.

The main objective of the programme is to mitigate the impacts of climate change on people, water, forests and cities, with significant objectives to build global climate change capacity and knowledge across the business. The partnership includes one of the largest employee engagement programmes on climate change, creating 'climate champions' worldwide who will be involved in research and spread their knowledge and experience across the business. Since launching the programme over 1500 employees have participated in local volunteering projects and nearly 150 have been trained as HSBC Climate Champions.

'At the end of the day,' concludes Williams, '[HSBC's] commitment to environmental best practice is as much enlightened self interest as it is an acknowledgement of [its] wider responsibility as a major business, employer and financial institution.'

Notes

1 In the 110th Congress (2007–2008) there have been 213 hearings held and 235 bills introduced dealing with climate change. The previous record for climate-related legislation was set by the 109th Congress, when 105 bills were introduced.
2 EPA modelling of the Lieberman–Warner Bill found that the inclusion of offsets reduced the price of allowances by 93 per cent.

References

Chicago Climate Exchange (CCX) (2007) 'Frequently asked questions', www.chicago-climatex.com

Elgin, B. (2007) 'Another inconvenient truth: Behind the feel-good hype of carbon offsets, some of the deals don't deliver', *Business Week*, 26 March

Energy Information Administration (EIA) (2007) 'Emissions of greenhouse gases', Report # DOE/EIA-0573(2006), November

IPCC (2007) 'IPCC fourth assessment report', IPCC, www.ipcc.ch/ipccreports/art.syr.htm

Stern, N. (2007) Stern Review on the economics of climate change', HM Treasury, www.hm-treasury.gov.uk/sternreview_index.htm

Hamilton, K., Sjardin, M., Marcello, T. and Xu, G. (2008) 'Forging a frontier: State of the voluntary carbon markets 2008', The Ecosystem Marketplace and New Carbon Finance, May

Trexler, M. C., Broekhoff, D. J. and Kosloff, L. H. (2006) 'A statistically-driven approach to offset-based GHG additionality determinations: What can we learn?', *Sustainable Development Law & Policy*, vol VI, pp30–40

US Environmental Protection Agency (EPA) (2008) 'EPA analysis of the Lieberman–Warner Climate Security Act of 2008', March, www.epa.gov/climatechange/downloads/s2191_EPA_Analysis.pdf

5

A Glance into the Future of the Voluntary Carbon Markets

Fifty years ago, the idea that markets would one day be used to protect the environment was little more than science fiction. Thirty years ago, a prediction that markets would one day help control acid rain would have been seen as fanciful. And five years ago, the thought that a European market in greenhouse gases (GHGs) would one day be worth nearly US$60 billion would have been considered ridiculous. And yet, all of this has come to pass. Yesterday's fiction is today's reality.

And so it may be with voluntary carbon markets. Today, the thought that there could one day be a large and thriving voluntary market in GHGs – a market where buyers and sellers transact in unseen gases without the threat of regulation – is easily dismissed. And yet, under most people's radar screens, voluntary carbon markets are growing and thriving. As German philosopher Arthur Schopenhauer (1788–1860) once said: 'All truth passes through three stages: First, it is ridiculed; second, it is violently opposed; and third, it is accepted as self-evident.'

Though it is not yet self-evident that the voluntary markets for GHGs will ever become large and robust, it is increasingly certain that these markets are growing at a rapid clip: from a few million tons three years ago to over 100 million tons in 2008.

A new outlet

In part, the growth of the voluntary carbon markets is but a reflection of the meteoric rise of the European and Kyoto carbon markets. As more and more money begins to move around in these compliance markets, some investors have begun to look for new and undiscovered outlets, for new and different carbon opportunities where the potential for growth is high and the level of competition is low. It should therefore come as no surprise that some are beginning to dip their toes into the growing tide of voluntary carbon transactions. It is still too soon to tell whether or not these bets will pay off. The point, however, is that people and organizations that four years ago would never have paid attention to a voluntary environmental market are today giving these markets a closer look.

Experienced carbon investors in Europe are not the only parties eyeing the voluntary carbon markets closely. Perhaps the greatest source of interest in the voluntary carbon markets has been driven by developments in the US. The last year has seen tremendous movement on the issue of climate change in the US. Not only has California passed climate change regulation that is likely to see the advent of a carbon market, but the states in the US northeast have created a carbon market of their own, while states in the west are talking about a large 'regional' climate initiative. Washington, DC is not far behind. Though the most significant carbon market regulation to date – the so-called Lieberman–Warner bill – was defeated in the US Senate in late summer 2008, there are more than two dozen similar laws being discussed in Congress and experts believe that a future Lieberman–Warner bill has a good chance of passing with the advent of a new administration in the US. As if that weren't enough, climate change has been the subject of cover stories in dozens of major US magazines (*Time, Elle, Wired, Vanity Fair*), as well as several feature films and numerous TV programmes (*An Inconvenient Truth*, CNN, Discovery Channel, CBS, etc.). As a result, the discussion has moved from one that asks 'Is climate change real?' to one that has begun to seek new ways to address what most now acknowledge is a serious problem. Public opinion, it would seem, is beginning to make the connection between increased storms, heat waves, droughts, hurricanes and global warming.

Since it looks as though political pressure may soon force the US to do something to address climate change – regardless of what happens in the next presidential election – there are those who feel that some form of carbon trading in the US cannot be far behind. Indeed, various analysts go further, claiming carbon trading in the US is inevitable and a national programme may even be put in place in the next two to five years.

Carbon markets, in short, are beginning to sprout in all shapes and forms across the US. And, since the country is one of the world's top two largest emitters (the other one being China) of GHGs, any markets that develop in the US could be relatively large.

Gourmet carbon

Judging from what is happening internationally, and especially in Europe and as a result of the Kyoto Protocol, the future will probably include both large compliance carbon markets and innovative and nimble (though relatively small) voluntary markets. These markets probably will occupy different niches, will attract different types of buyers and sellers, and will look and feel different. Some of these differences are obvious: lots of bureaucracy, lots of money and larger players in the regulated market; smaller players, more involved transactions and more variety in the voluntary market.

Some differences, however, are perhaps less obvious: buyer types and buyer preferences, for instance, will probably be different in each of these markets. In a market where buyers are only interested in complying with regulations and where credits are completely fungible, buyers will naturally gravitate towards those credits with the least cost. If this means looking towards reducing pollution in large industries and destroying hydrofluorocarbons in China, so be it. Buyers in the voluntary markets, on the other hand, are likely to be a bit pickier about the carbon they end up buying. Since buyers are in this game voluntarily, they will be looking for the carbon that will give them the biggest political, public relations and/or 'ethical' bang for their buck. In a way, this is understandable: companies engaging in carbon offsetting for public relations purposes and individuals offsetting their emissions for ethical reasons want to be able to justify their actions easily; they want to feel good about the carbon they are buying. In the case of companies, they also want their carbon purchases to contribute towards risk management. For them, the destruction of exotic gases in large industrial parks in China is less appealing than installing solar panels in Bangladesh, or planting forests somewhere closer to where their customers live.

In other words, whereas the regulated markets are following the age-old evolution of markets towards the commoditization of a good or service – they are creating a form of commodity carbon, where a ton is a ton is a ton, no matter the source – the voluntary markets appear to be gravitating towards a value-added model; one that seeks to provide what we might call 'gourmet carbon', where the provenance and feel-good attributes of the carbon play an increasingly important role.

The commodity carbon vs gourmet carbon divide has implications for the price elasticity of carbon offsets in the two markets. Where carbon is simply a commodity, prices will be driven to their lowest possible level; they will be determined largely by the costs of production and their ability to provide compliance (i.e. meet the standards established by regulators); and they will tend to deviate less from some fixed point of reference (such as the price of carbon on a given exchange). By contrast, where carbon is bought for its various attributes, where price is not the only factor, and where people have their heart set on projects that simply feel good, the price will probably fluctuate across a larger band, based largely on budgets, on consumer preference, and on the supply of similar projects available to the market. As the markets become more standardized, and as voluntary carbon commodities such as the Voluntary Carbon Unit (VCU) enter the markets, this might change slightly, but a tension between industrial buyers and speculators, who want a fungible commodity, and other buyers, whose main interest is the overall feel of the projects they are funding, likely will remain. This would seem to suggest that, even with the advent of standardization schemes, there will always be a market for carbon with additional certifications and assurances of provenance – a kind of Appellation d'Origine Contrôlée in the voluntary market.

The broad spectrum

Pushed and pulled by different buyers with different needs, the voluntary markets may one day split themselves into two main segments: one large, more commoditized market aimed at speculators and large companies interested in offering standardized climate neutrality with their products; and one smaller, more idiosyncratic market aimed at individuals and companies interested in specific types of offset projects (e.g. trees, community development and/or renewable energy). In the first market, there will be a kind of currency (like the VCU or Verified Emissions Reduction (VER)) that gets traded and ensures quality, helps provide risk management and generates political cover. In the second market, offset projects will be differentiated by type, provenance and their provision of 'co-benefits' to the environment and/or to local communities.

If the buyers end up being mostly large corporations wanting to brand their products as carbon neutral, then standardization of the market (see Appendix 3) will become increasingly likely. If, however, the buyers are overwhelmingly individuals and corporations simply wishing to give themselves a green image, then the market will tend to focus mostly on value added and will follow the gourmet carbon approach – where carbon comes in many different looks and flavours. Again, it may not be an either/or scenario. It is quite possible – maybe even probable – that both types of buyer will coexist within one market. In that case, we could imagine a situation where carbon is certified to a certain level, a floor, and then has additional certifications or branding based on its various co-benefits (e.g. is it good for communities, for biodiversity, does it come from Mexico, China, the US, etc.). In a way, this means that parts of the voluntary carbon markets will come to resemble the compliance carbon market, and parts will diverge significantly.

Perhaps we should look at them as part of a broader spectrum of carbon markets ranging from compliance commoditized markets, through voluntary commoditized markets, all the way to voluntary gourmet markets.

Unanswered questions

At the same time as interest is growing in the broad spectrum of carbon markets, initiatives to standardize and certify voluntary carbon offsets have begun to take shape, suggesting that a self-reinforcing cycle of growth, attention and interest in voluntary carbon has started to move.

And yet, many questions remain. Even though the voluntary carbon markets may be bigger – and more profitable – than anyone would have imagined five years ago, it is also becoming clear that these markets are not without complications, and that further growth will not be possible unless certain fundamental issues are addressed.

How will the voluntary markets interact with the regulated carbon markets and with other existing environmental markets? Will the demand for voluntary carbon prove sustainable, and if so, what will drive it? Will voluntary carbon offsets be standardized in ways that will help the market grow? And, if so, will it be done in ways that negate some of the voluntary market's greatest strengths (innovation, flexibility and the ability to include communities in developing countries)? Last, but certainly not least, will the voluntary markets deliver on their promise to *help* tackle climate change?

This publication has sought to ask all of these questions and to weigh answers to some of them, but we readily acknowledge that there are no definitive answers yet because they depend on political choices that have yet to be made, and on the behaviour of thousands of individual and corporate buyers.

Moving towards answers

What we can already say is that the voluntary carbon markets are rapidly becoming an interesting public relations and risk management option for companies, at the same time as they help involve and educate consumers about the importance of combating climate change. Already, these markets are providing the sort of innovation and flexibility that is simply not possible via the regulated markets. They are allowing more types of people to participate in carbon trading, and they are allowing more types of offsets to be sold.

On the issue of voluntary vs regulatory, we think that the voluntary carbon markets will find a way to coexist with regulated carbon markets. We think this coexistence can and should be beneficial to all concerned, with the voluntary markets helping to fill gaps in the regulated markets. And we think voluntary markets should not be seen as alternatives to regulated markets, but rather as supplements; supplements that can help educate and engage broad sectors of society in the fight against climate change, and that can help provide the sort of flexibility, inclusiveness and innovation that will become increasingly necessary if we are to address climate change. The question of voluntary vs regulatory is, therefore, nothing but a false dichotomy.

Where the issue of voluntary vs regulatory markets does get interesting, however, is in the interaction between voluntary carbon markets and regulatory (as well as voluntary) markets for renewable energy certificates, or RECs. We have devoted an entire chapter of this book to this issue because we see it as a potential source of pain and complication on both sides. Currently, the market for RECs and the fledgling markets for carbon (at least in the US) have been somewhat conflated. On the one side, both buyers and sellers of RECs advertise and justify their activities in terms of carbon emission reductions. On the other, sellers of voluntary carbon are often selling RECs as a substitute for carbon emission reductions. So what happens once there is a more robust market for carbon? Does a large part of the market for RECs get subsumed into the carbon market? Does this kill the REC market, or does it just force it to change shape?

Niels Bohr, the Nobel prize-winning physicist is said to have quipped: 'Prediction is very difficult, especially if it's about the future.' This caveat notwithstanding, our prediction is that parts of the REC market will be subsumed into the carbon markets, and parts will remain outside of it. The parts that will most likely remain impervious to the carbon markets will probably be the regulated REC markets, with much of the voluntary REC market using the carbon markets as a convenient outlet.

On the issue of demand, we believe that there will be two distinct (and somewhat different) sources of demand for voluntary carbon. One source will come from individuals and institutions interested in playing a role in addressing climate change. The size of this particular customer base is currently hard to gauge, since it will depend to a large extent on how the climate change problem continues to be perceived by the general public. It will also depend somewhat on whether or not people feel governments are doing enough to address the problem. The second source of demand is likely to be corporations and institutions that feel compelled – for a variety of reasons – to go beyond regulation to address climate change. Here again, the size of this market will depend on public opinion and the ultimate scope of government regulation. In other words, if companies feel that their consumers expect them to become climate neutral, if there appears to be a preference in the market (or some other business case) for climate neutrality, then companies will be in the market for offsets. The scope of regulation is important here, too, because if climate regulation is believed to be exceedingly strict, or if it is seen by all as being sufficient to address the perceived problem, then there will be little incentive to participate in a voluntary market.

Additionally, it is important to note that these two potential sources of demand will likely have two very different approaches towards buying carbon. Large buyers will want to minimize transaction costs and ensure adequate levels of risk management. For this reason they are likely to push for standardization and a further commoditization of voluntary carbon. This could lead to rapid growth (in terms of volume) of the voluntary markets, but it could, at the same time, mean more money being spent on certification and verification, and less money making it down to the original supplier of the emissions reduction credit. This is a trend we have seen with many other commodities: from coffee and sugar to corn and pork bellies.

Smaller individual buyers, on the other hand, will have a different approach towards buying carbon. They will be in the market for gourmet carbon – carbon that has various other beneficial qualities, whether they be environmental, social or otherwise. In the market for gourmet carbon, the price will depend on the qualities of the carbon being offered, and sellers will seek to 'brand', 'certify', or otherwise make the carbon they have to offer palatable to these consumers.

On the issue of standardization, we believe that large parts of the voluntary carbon market will become increasingly standardized, but we hope this standardization is done in such a way that it does not effectively prevent small producers in developing countries from entering the markets. We hope that the search for confidence, certainty and fungibility does not take away from the flexibility, innovation and inclusiveness that is such a hallmark of the voluntary carbon markets. To do this, we feel it is important for those developing standards for voluntary carbon not to be unnecessarily restrictive in the types of carbon offsets that can be considered, and that they come up with inexpensive and cost-effective ways of ensuring and verifying additionality; ways that don't impose too onerous a cost on offset project developers. In all likelihood, this will require the creation and use of in-country certifiers and verifiers.

In this, there is perhaps an interesting role for philanthropic donors to play – as funders of the training of in-country carbon certifiers, or perhaps in the creation of a 'certifier of certifiers' approach such as that which is undertaken via the Forest Stewardship Council. Either way, this is an issue that needs to be quickly resolved. For it would be a shame if the old chestnut of the agricultural community – that there is money to made in food, just not from growing it – were to one day apply to offset project providers in developing countries.

Finally, we believe the issue of quality will be an ongoing and never-ending battle for the voluntary carbon markets, and that the pendulum will forever swing from the desire for ever-greater assurances of the quality of offsets (and therefore rigour in certification) on the one side, to the desire for lower transaction costs, more innovation, and inclusiveness (and therefore simpler certification mechanisms) on the other. Currently the market is experiencing a strong push towards greater rigour and greater assurances of product quality. This is as it should be. For too long the market has operated with little or no emphasis on quality – a trend that could, if taken too far, seriously dampen (if not quell) the market's potential for growth.

Overall, however, we would argue that the future of voluntary carbon markets looks bright. As storms – literal, figurative and political – batter the concept of climate change into the public consciousness, companies, governments and concerned citizens will begin to look for simple and creative solutions to this global problem. In doing so, they will inevitably turn to markets, one of the most cost-effective and proven tools for reducing emissions of an atmospheric pollutant.

Even if the voluntary carbon markets do not mature into a truly robust marketplace, they will remain a source of innovation, inspiration, and education. They will also continue to serve as an interesting barometer of public opinion and businesses weighing options for branding and risk management. If the massive clouds that made up the numerous hurricanes that struck around the world in 2004 and 2005 had a silver lining, it was this: they helped breathe new life into a global market in voluntary carbon emissions reductions that, one way or another, will play an important role in our efforts to stem climate change for years to come.

References

Kenber, M. (2006) Presentation at GreenT Forum: Raising the Bar for Voluntary Environmental Credit Markets, New York, 1–2 May

Appendix 1

Offset Project Types

One major variation among carbon credits is the origin of the credit. As described in Chapter 2, carbon credits take the form of either rights to pollute (allowances) or project-based greenhouse gas (GHG) emissions reductions (offsets). With the exception of credits traded on the CCX and credits retired from the regulatory market, all credits in the voluntary sector originate from offset projects.

Offset projects generate carbon credits by reducing any of the six GHGs identified by the Kyoto Protocol: carbon dioxide, methane, nitrous oxide, sulphur hexafluoride, hydrofluorocarbons and perfluorocarbons. Projects can be classified into three main categories: those that reduce the occurrence of GHG-emitting activities, those that destroy GHGs and those that reduce GHG levels in the atmosphere via sequestration. Each category can then be further classified into project types, with some projects – such as avoided deforestation or 'REDD' (Reduced Emissions from Deforestation and Degradation) projects – spanning two categories (See Figure A1.1)

Recognizing that there are a wide variety of means of generating carbon credits, this section focuses on the most widely used sources of offset credits in the voluntary markets. It is important to note that many of the different advantages and disadvantages mentioned in this section are project- and situation-specific; the goal of this section is to generalize for the purpose of comparison.

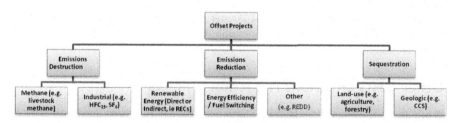

Figure A1.1 *Common emission reduction and sequestration project categories*

Emissions reduction projects

Fossil fuel emissions reduction projects

The burning of fossil fuels is the leading cause of human-generated GHG emissions; therefore, reducing the use of fossil fuels is critical to decelerating the rate of climate change. As described in Chapter 3, projects may reduce the use of fossil fuel directly or indirectly. Projects reducing emissions directly do so at the source. They include energy efficiency projects, fuel switches, power plant upgrades and off-grid renewable energy projects, such as small-scale hydro, wind and biomass. For example, the Climate Trust creates offsets generated by a paper manufacturing efficiency project, which reduces CO_2 emissions over a 'business-as-usual' scenario by utilizing recycled paper feedstocks and equipment retrofits to increase the energy efficiency of the manufacturing process. The Solar Electric Light Fund (SELF) generates emissions reductions from solar energy projects that replace diesel generators in countries around the world, from Nigeria to the Solomon Islands. (See Chapter 3 for more information on the differences between these renewable energy projects and Renewable Energy Certificates (RECs).)

Fossil fuel reduction projects offer several important benefits in addition to GHG emission reduction. They often result in numerous environmental and human health co-benefits by avoiding the generation of air pollutants such as carbon monoxide, nitrous oxide (another GHG), nitrogen dioxide, particulate matter and sulphur dioxide. Reducing fossil fuel use may also provide national security benefits by way of decreasing dependence on fossil fuels, 'green' job creation, incentivizing technology transfer among countries and long-term cost savings (via energy efficiency projects). Small off-grid renewable energy projects may offer the additional benefit of reduced deforestation by relieving pressure on wood-based fuel sources.

These benefits notwithstanding, generating credits via fossil fuel reductions is relatively inefficient from a financial lens, as the return on investment generated by other types is sometimes much greater. Flaring methane (a gas with a global warming potential (GWP) 23 times that of CO_2) over a 100-year period or destroying HFC-23 (a gas with a GWP 11,700 times that of CO_2) over a 100-year period, for instance, has to date generated far more credits per dollar invested. However, as the supply of these 'low hanging fruit' industrial gas projects dwindles, the share of renewable energy and energy efficiency projects in the voluntary market has soared, boosting the opportunity to take advantage of their co-benefits.

Other GHG emissions reduction projects

While fossil fuel-based GHG emissions projects are the most common type of emissions reduction project in the voluntary markets, credits can also be created by avoiding the release of other GHGs, such the industrial gaess perfluorocarbon

(PFC) and sulphur hexafluoride (SF_6), which are produced in the manufacture of semiconductors and in aluminum/electronics manufacturing, respectively.

Also included in this 'other' category are emissions reductions generated by avoided deforestation, or 'REDD', projects. REDD (Reduced Emissions from Deforestation and Degradation) is a unique sector because it overlaps with the sequestration category. Similar to the concept of avoiding GHG emissions by avoiding fossil fuel burning, REDD projects generate emissions reductions via the conservation of forests at risk of deforestation, thereby avoiding the CO_2 emissions that would have been released. Environmentalists have pointed to REDD projects as an immediate option to compensate for 20 per cent of human-induced GHG emissions, and market activity suggests that their share of the voluntary market may increase in coming years. At the same time, REDD projects are more controversial than most other project types (because of permanence threats and the difficulty of measuring leakage and setting baselines) and have, to date, not been a major project subcategory in the voluntary scene.

Emissions destruction projects

Unlike CO_2, gases such as methane can be captured and flared into less potent GHGs, reducing their GWP, and sometimes used as sources of electricity. Projects involving methane destruction are the most common GHG destruction projects in the voluntary markets, especially in the retail market. However, credits from the destruction of other potent GHGs such as hydrofluorocarbons (HFCs) are also available.

Methane projects

Both Certified Emissions Reductions (CERs) and Verified Emissions Reductions (VERs) have been produced by capturing and flaring methane from landfills, livestock manure 'lagoons' and coal mines. Methane offset projects are extremely popular due to methane's high GWP and because captured methane can also be used to generate renewable energy for on- or off-grid purposes. Hence, in some cases, a methane project may create two streams of revenue: one from the sale of the direct methane destruction and the other from the sale of an REC. Generating electricity from methane projects can also increase the project's return on investment to the extent that carbon financing is not deemed a necessary incentive for project creation.

Livestock

In large-scale livestock activities, especially pig and dairy farming, animal manure is liquefied and stored in large, often open lagoons. These lagoons emit strong odours, methane and ammonia. The manure is often spread on fields for fertilizer, resulting in emissions of CO_2 and nitrous oxide (N_2O), as well as excessive nutrient discharges in local water (Amey, 2005).

Techniques for methane recovery include of the use of anaerobic digesters in covered lagoons (www.methanetomarkets.org). Once captured, methane is flared and then sometimes used by the farmer to fuel farm operations. The numerous co-benefits resulting from livestock methane projects are a comparative advantage over other methane projects (Barbour, 2006). One social co-benefit of livestock methane projects that doesn't apply as extensively to landfill or coal mine projects is reduced odour. Environmental benefits include reduced ammonia (a precursor to the air pollutant PM10), and reduced groundwater contamination due to minimizing the risk that the lagoons will overflow manure into local drinking water (Kunz, 2006). Manure may be spread on fields post-methane removal, further reducing the chance of groundwater contamination via lagoon overflow.

Landfills

According to the Methane to Markets Partnership, a voluntary international initiative created to advance the recovery and use of methane, landfills accounted for 8 per cent of global methane emissions in 2008. Decomposing matter emits landfill gas, which is about 50 per cent methane and about 50 per cent CO_2. If trapped and flared, however, the methane component can be converted into a source of energy, providing climate change mitigation and energy sustainability benefits.

The US and Europe have required that large landfills be covered and methane emissions flared. Landfills in many developing countries, however, are generally exempt from such regulation and as such, landfill gas projects in developing countries often fulfil the regulatory additionality test for high quality voluntary credits. Co-benefits from landfill projects in general can be considered less substantial than benefits from livestock. They include some level of reduced odour and often a reduced likelihood of pollutants leaching into groundwater.

Coal mines

In 2008, coal mining accounted for 4 per cent of total global methane emissions resulting from human activities. Both active and abandoned mines release methane (Methane to Markets, 2008). Due to the potential for built-up methane to cause explosions, laws require the removal of methane from active mines around the world. The cheapest method for removing methane from mines is to release it into the air through vents, but such a release does nothing to reduce its atmospheric concentration.

As with livestock and landfill methane, coal mine methane can be trapped to generate electricity and/or flared to reduce its global warming potency. Compared to landfill and livestock operations, the co-benefits from this process are fairly minimal (Kunz, 2006), but methane capture projects may lead to updated safety mechanisms that transcend business-as-usual requirements, especially in developing countries.

Industrial GHG destruction

Like methane, trifluoromethane (HFC-23) and nitrous oxide (N_2O) are Kyoto-regulated gases that can be destroyed. HFCs are often used to replace chlorofluorocarbons (CFCs), the internationally regulated ozone-depleting GHGs, in many applications, such as refrigeration. While HFCs are not ozone depleting and generally have a lower GWP than CFCs, they are still powerful GHGs, with 100-year GWPs of between 140 and 11,700 (EPA, 2008a). N_2O is another powerful GHG with a global warming potential 320 times higher than CO_2. Major sources of N_2O include agricultural activities, fossil fuel combustion, nitric acid production and solid waste burning.

While projects generating emissions reductions of both HFC-23 and N_2O are eligible to produce credits on the CCX market, and there is also approved methodology for their destruction under the Clean Development Mechanism (CDM), sales of credits from HFC-23 occur mostly on the wholesale market and remain particularly rare in the retail market.

Sequestration projects

Sequestration projects pull CO_2 out of the air or, as in the case of REDD projects, avoid the release of already-sequestered CO_2, much like energy efficiency projects avoid the release of CO_2 from fossil fuels. Sequestration-based projects aim to increase the number and productivity of (often natural) carbon sinks in forests, oceans and agricultural soils. Within the sinks category, two types of projects currently source credits into the voluntary markets: 'biological' land-use projects (e.g. forestry and soil) and 'technological' (geological sequestration) projects. Land-use projects, especially those involving forestry, are far more common sources of carbon credits than technological projects in the voluntary market.

Under the Kyoto Protocol, land-use projects are referred to as 'Land Use, Land-Use Change and Forestry' (LULUCF) projects. Under the Voluntary Carbon Standard, they are referred to as Agriculture, Forestry and Other Land Use (AFOLU). As of the publication of this book, six voluntary carbon standards had produced project protocols for forestry projects, and it is expected that more standards will release forestry protocols in the next few months.

Land-use projects

The role of land-based projects has been hotly debated in both the regulatory and voluntary carbon markets, with perceptions changing significantly in only a couple of years. For example, the CDM board has approved some afforestation/reforestation methodologies but has not yet approved any REDD methodologies; international UN climate negotiations suggest that REDD methodologies will soon be eligible to generate emissions reduction credits in the Kyoto offset markets.

Proponents of land-based projects note that while sequestration projects are not permanent, they offer a mechanism for immediately decelerating the quantity of GHGs entering the atmosphere and can help mitigate climate change during this transitional period of low carbon technology development. One supporter of land-based carbon projects, Patrick Zimmerman, Director of the Institute of Atmospheric Sciences at the South Dakota School of Mines and Technology, summarizes his view this way: 'Is it permanent? No. Is it important? You bet it's important' (Zimmerman, 2006).

Forestry projects

The early voluntary offset transactions were based around forestry projects. Deforestation contributes an estimated 20–25 per cent of anthropogenic GHGs to the atmosphere. Hence, projects that lead to more global forest cover clearly play a role in GHG mitigation. However, forestry is one of the more controversial project types in the voluntary carbon markets. Critics point out the difficulty of measuring baselines, evaluating leakage potential and protecting against permanence risks.

Proponents of forestry projects in the voluntary market cite not only their clear role in sequestering CO_2, but also the numerous co-benefits of forestry projects. Well-managed forestry projects can contribute to biological diversity, increased forest productivity, reduced erosion, hydrological regulation and economic development. Furthermore, because most consumers have been exposed to the carbon cycle at some point in their education, forestry offsets are one of the easiest types of sequestration projects for consumers to understand.

Denis Slieker, Director of Netherlands-based offset provider Business for Climate, notes, 'One reason people want forests is because [they are] tangible ... [They] also ha[ve] an emotional aspect. [They] not only help the climate, [they're] also a home for the animals and community development.'

Erica Keeley, Offset Portfolio Manager for The Climate Trust, observes, 'There are a lot of co-benefits to using carbon money to fund reforestation as far as air, biodiversity and water quality goes but there's also a lot of risk associated with it.' Presenting the most significant risk is the question of permanence. 'You cannot guarantee that the trees will still be there in 40 years if there's a forest fire or logging,' notes MyClimate's Corinne Moser (Biello, 2005). This uncertainty becomes particularly critical for accurate carbon accounting, and permanence risks have presented a major roadblock for forestry project headway in the regulated markets.

Forestry sinks also give rise to questions about leakage – the notion that the activity bringing about an emissions reduction in one area will give rise to an emissions increase in another. In the case of forestry projects, critics point out that it is difficult to guarantee that transforming agricultural land into forest in one area will not drive clear-cutting to provide land for farming somewhere else.

Forestry projects may utilize '*ex post*' (after the reductions occur) or '*ex ante*' (before the reductions occur) accounting. Financing the initial cost of a forestry project, especially a reforestation or afforestation project, is risky, as the investor always runs the risk that the emissions reductions may not take place (Burnett, 2006).

Last but not least, large monoculture forestry projects – attractive to project developers because they generate emissions reductions relatively quickly and cost-effectively – may not offer the co-benefits provided by indigenous forests. Monocrop plantations in the tropics are especially appealing to developers, as they support fast-growing trees such as Klinki. However, critics note that many of these projects contribute little to biodiversity conservation, and may even reduce water supplies or have negative social impacts. Brett Orlando, climate change adviser at the IUCN in Switzerland, summarizes: 'The question is, will sequestration be maximized at the expense of other social and environmental objectives? Carbon sequestration is just one of the services that forests provide' (Nicholls, 2005).

Soil projects

Carbon offsets from soil sequestration are far less common in the over-the-counter (OTC) carbon market, but they constitute a major portion of credits on the CCX. In the US, federal agencies have prepared an extensive methodology for calculating emissions reductions from land-based agricultural projects. In 'conservation tillage', which includes no-till, minimal till, ridge till and mulch till farming, crop residues are left on the fields after harvesting to increase the amount of carbon stored in soils. Co-benefits include reduced soil erosion, reduced energy-related emissions reductions from farm equipment, and increased soil organic content (EPA, 2008b).

Critics of agricultural sequestration have noted that agricultural carbon projects generally would not pass a 'financial' additionality test because they do not capture enough carbon to provide a necessary financial incentive for changing farming practices. More importantly from an atmospheric perspective, projects may offer even less permanency than forestry projects. The carbon sequestered can be quickly lost in a season when a farmer changes tilling practices (Barbour, 2006).

Proponents of obtaining offsets from agricultural management practices counter that it is important to send the price signal to farmers that no/low-till farming can be a desirable alternative to traditional agriculture. Like forests, they say, the soil represents a major carbon sink; deep ploughing techniques can be equated to 'mining the soil for carbon' (Barbour, 2006).

Geological sequestration: Carbon capture and sequestration

Geologic sequestration projects involve storing CO_2 deep beneath the earth's surface in geologic formations for long periods of time. The practice of injecting CO_2 into subsurface features has been used for years for enhanced oil and gas recovery, but the technology for long-term carbon sequestration is more complicated and very expensive, resulting in relatively few Carbon

Capture and Storage (CCS) projects sourcing credits into the voluntary markets to date.

CCS projects involve capturing CO_2 from stationary sources (such as coal-fired power plants or industrial facilities), piping it to a geologic site (usually a depleted oil or gas reservoir), and storing it in these (usually natural) geologic features. In 2007 credits from CCS projects comprised only 1 per cent of the transacted voluntary market volume (Hamilton et al, 2008), and in researching for this book, the authors found only one organization selling CCS credits into the market. This organization, Blue Source (in partnership with Natsource), has sold credits from captured waste CO_2 injected into fields to access hard-to-reach oil reserves.

Despite the national security potential of CCS technology to yield more domestically produced oil, critics cite numerous disadvantages associated with using CCS technology to source voluntary carbon credits. For one, CCS projects may be profitable without carbon finance (because of profits from oil or gas recovery, for instance), and as such, they will likely fail the investment additionality test (see Chapter 2 for more on 'additionality'). Second, some critics have argued that the process feeds developed countries' 'addictions to fossil fuel'. Third, there are few environmental or social co-benefits associated with the effort.

References

Barbour, W. Interviewed by Kate Hamilton, 6 May 2006

Biello, D. (2005) 'Speaking for the trees', *The Ecosystem Marketplace*, www.ecosystem marketplace.com

EPA (US Environmental Protection Agency) (2008a) 'High global warming potential (GWP) gases', www.epa.gov/highgwp/ag.html

EPA (US Environmental Protection Agency) (2008b) 'Agricultural practices that sequester carbon and/or reduce emissions of other greenhouse gases', last updated 19 October 2008, www.epa.gov/sequestration/ag.html

Hamilton, K., Sjardin, M., Marcello, T. and Xu, G. (2008) 'Forging a frontier: State of the voluntary carbon markets 2008', The Ecosystem Marketplace and New Carbon Finance, May

IPCC (2005) 'Second Assessment Report', www.ipcc.ch/pub/reports.htm

Kunz, J. Interviewed by Kate Hamilton, 7 May 2006

Methane to Markets (2008) 'Coal mine background information', http://methaneto markets.org/coalmines/coalmines-bkgrd.htm

Metz, B. et al (eds) (2005) *Carbon Dioxide Capture and Storage: Special Report of the Intergovernmental Panel on Climate Change (IPCC)*, Cambridge University Press, Cambridge

Nicholls, M. (2005) 'Credits for sinks', *The Ecosystem Marketplace*, www.ecosystem marketplace.com

Zimmerman, P. (2006) 'The quality challenge: Are all credits created equal?' Speech given at The GreenT Forum: Raising the Bar for Voluntary Environmental Credit Markets, New York, 1 May

Offset Standards

This appendix outlines the major voluntary carbon offset standards around the world and then compares key differences between them. Voluntary offset standards can be separated into several categories: accounting protocols, programmes that certify offset projects and carbon credits, and programmes that implement protocols and certify companies or products. Some standards do not fit neatly into a single category and can therefore be defined as occupying more than one category.

Additionally, some companies utilize their own set of screens or standards for both developing offset projects and deciding which offsets are viable purchases. In some cases suppliers have branded such standards or made them publicly available. For example, in 2007 General Electric (GE) and AES joined forces to launch a Greenhouse Gas Services venture with its own Standard of Practice (Greenhouse Gas Services, 2008). This standard is available for third party use, but is currently still utilized primarily by the founding company.

It is important to note that the Chicago Climate Exchange (CCX) has its own standards and hence represents an offset standard within the CCX market. CCX standards are compared with others but not discussed again in this section. For more information on any of the standards, please consult their websites, provided at the end of this appendix.

Project Standards

California Climate Action Registry's Climate Action Reserve

The California Climate Action Registry (CCAR) was established by Californian statute as a non-profit voluntary registry for GHG emissions. Over the last four years, CCAR has developed project protocols that allow for the quantification and certification of GHG emission reductions. These protocols now serve as a 'verifiable' quasi-standard for voluntary carbon offsets. In mid-2008, CCAR launched the Climate Action Reserve (CAR), co-developed with APX Inc, which serves as a registry for credits verified to the CCAR protocols and will create more project protocols. Currently, CAR has approved protocols for forestry, landfill gas, livestock and urban forestry projects. The Registry is evaluating protocols for seven additional project types ranging from truck stop electrification to tidal wetland restoration. The CCAR protocols became particularly relevant in the US voluntary carbon market in 2007, when the California Air Resources Board, directed by California's Assembly Bill (AB) 32 to design a mechanism for reducing emissions, formally endorsed CCAR's forest sector project protocols as eligible carbon offset project types.

CarbonFix Standard

The CarbonFix Standard (CFS) was launched in late 2007 and only pertains to forestry projects. Adherence to the CFS requires third party certification from CFS-approved auditors. CFS emphasizes sustainable forestry management and ensures that CFS carbon credits are derived from projects maintained in such a manner. The CFS aims to operate in a transparent manner, posting all documents online except for financial calculations and the prices of CO_2 certificates sold. CFS also provides customers with a way to purchase CFS certified credits on its website directly from project developers, charging a fee of 3 per cent of the sales price.

Chicago Climate Exchange Offsets Program

The Chicago Climate Exchange (CCX) has its own standards for offset projects accepted into the voluntary cap-and-trade system. To screen applicants, the exchange has standardized rules for seven different types of projects: agricultural methane, landfill methane, agricultural soil carbon, forestry, renewable energy, coal mine methane and rangeland soil carbon management. Requirements for each project type are outlined on the CCX website. One screening criteria, for instance, is project start date; agricultural methane or soil carbon projects initiated after 1999 or forestation projects initiated after 1990 may qualify as approved offsets. Projects that meet initial screening criteria may submit proposals to the CCX Committee on Offsets for review and preliminary approval. After approval, all project developers must obtain independent verification from an approved third party verifier before registering offset credits on the exchange.

Climate, Community and Biodiversity Standards

The Climate, Community, and Biodiversity Standards (CCB Standards) are a set of project-design criteria for evaluating land-based carbon mitigation projects and their community and biodiversity co-benefits. These standards can be applied to Clean Development Mechanism (CDM) or voluntary market projects. The development of the CCB Standards was spearheaded by the Climate, Community and Biodiversity Alliance (CCBA), an international partnership of corporations, research institutions and non-governmental organizations (NGOs) such as Conservation International, The Nature Conservancy,

Weyerhauser, Intel and CATIE. As a 'project design' standard, CCB Standards can be used at the project-design phase for third party validation that the project has the potential to produce not only emissions reduction credits, but also community and biodiversity benefits. The CCB Standards also provide a means of verifying these benefits once a project is being implemented, but they do not include their own carbon accounting standard at this time. The CCBA therefore recommends that the CCB Standards be applied on top of an existing standard designed for carbon accounting, such as the CDM or the Voluntary Carbon Standard (VCS).

Greenhouse Friendly

Greenhouse Friendly is the Australian government's voluntary carbon offset pro-gramme for encouraging GHG emissions reductions at several levels, including 'providing businesses and consumers with the opportunity to sell and purchase greenhouse-neutral products and services'. The initiative provides two different services: Greenhouse Friendly Abatement Provider (offset project) certification and certification of 'carbon neutral' products and services.

Criteria for Greenhouse Friendly project certification include: being Australia-based, generating 'additional, permanent and verifiable greenhouse gas emission reductions or sequestration', and 'clearly demonstrating that the abate-ment generated is additional to business as usual'. Greenhouse Friendly 'carbon-neutral' accreditation requires the preparation of an independently verified life cycle assessment, an emissions monitoring plan, annual reports and the use of Greenhouse Friendly approved carbon offsets.

The Gold Standard for Verified Emissions Reductions (VERs)

The Gold Standard seeks to define the high-end market for carbon credits aris-ing from renewable energy and energy efficiency projects that contribute signif-icantly to sustainable development. The standard specifically excludes forestry and land-use projects. The Gold Standard was an initiative of the World Wildlife Fund (WWF) and was developed with a variety of other NGOs, businesses and governmental organizations who believed that the Kyoto Clean Development Mechanism did not adequately screen projects for their contributions to sus-tainable development. While the Gold Standard was originally created to sup-plement CDM projects, it now also certifies voluntary offset projects. In 2008, the Standard joined forces with the private firm APX to develop and manage the Gold Standard VER registry.

ISO 14064/65 standards

The ISO 14064/65 standards are part of the International Organization for Standardization (ISO) family of standards. The protocol currently includes four components:

- **Organization reporting**: Guiding organizations' quantification and reporting of GHG emissions (ISO 14964 Part 1).
- **Project reporting**: Guiding project proponents' quantification, monitoring and reporting of GHG emissions reductions (ISO 14064 Part 2).
- **Validation and verification**: Guiding the validation and verification of GHG assertions from organizations or projects (ISO 14064 Part 3).
- **Accreditation of validation and verification bodies**: Guiding the accreditation or recognition of competent GHG validation or verification bodies (ISO 14064 Part 4).

Much like the World Resource Institute / World Business Council for Sustainable Development's (WRI/WBCSD) GHG Protocol, the ISO standards were not created to support a particular kind of GHG reduction programme, but were instead designed to be 'regime neutral' so that they could be used as the basis for any programme. Unlike the WRI/WBCSD GHG Protocol, which specifically includes tools and accounting methods, ISO 14064 does not spell out the exact requirements. ISO does not certify or register GHG emissions or credits, but the ISO 14064 does certify institutions who abide by these principles. For example, the Australian Greenhouse Challenge Plus voluntary reduction programme utilizes ISO standards as a foundation (Zwick, 2006).

Plan Vivo

Plan Vivo is a standard specifically designed for community-based agroforestry projects that describes itself as 'a system for promoting sustainable livelihoods in rural communities, through the creation of verifiable carbon credits'. The system was created eight years ago by the Edinburgh Centre for Carbon Management (ECCM) and is now managed by the non-profit organization BioClimate Research and Development (BR&D). Plan Vivo currently has three fully operational projects in Mexico, Uganda and Mozambique that are generating emission reductions via carbon sequestration for sale as Plan Vivo-verified carbon offsets. According to the organization's website, the Plan Vivo system aims to ensure that its projects deliver the following benefits: social benefits, biodiversity benefits, transparency, additionality, foundations for permanence, an ethical option, and scientific and technical partnerships.

Social Carbon

The Social Carbon methodology and certification programme is created and owned by the Brazilian NGO Ecológica. The methodology is based on a sustainable livelihoods approach focused on improving 'project effectiveness by using an integrated approach which values local communities, cares for peoples' potential and resources, and takes account for existing power relations and political context'. The methodology was first created to ensure 'higher quality Kyoto Protocol carbon projects'. However, the programme methodology is now also used for voluntary market projects. The Social Carbon methodology has been used in hydrology, fuel switching and forestry projects in Latin America and Portugal since 2000. The Ecológica Institute plans to release a registry for Social Carbon projects in mid-2008. Recently, the NGO also launched the for-profit Social Carbon Company, which donates a percentage of its profits back to Ecológica. While the company was created to develop and sell credits from Social Carbon projects, the Social Carbon standard is still designed to remain a third party standard that can be licensed by any project developer.

VER+ Standard

In May 2007, project verifier TÜV SÜD announced the launch of its VER+ Standard, which certifies both carbon neutrality and carbon credits from voluntary offset projects. Martin Schröder of TÜV SÜD describes the standard as 'streamlined' Kyoto because the standard closely follows the CDM and Joint Implementation (JI) methodology. In tandem with VER+, TÜV SÜD also created the Blue Registry, which serves as the VER+ Registry and aims eventually to be a platform for managing VERs from a variety of other standards, including the CCX offset programme and the VCS.

Voluntary Carbon Standard

The latest version of the VCS was launched in November 2007 by the Climate Group, the International Emissions Trading Association and the World Economic Forum. The VCS aims to standardize, increase fungibility and stimulate innovation in the voluntary offset market. Mark Kenber, Policy Director at The Climate Group, described the standard as creating a basic 'quality threshold' in the market. Credits certified via the VCS are then called Voluntary Carbon Units (VCUs). Version 1 of the VCS was released in March 2006 as both a consultation document and a pilot standard for use in the market. The final version of the standard, called 'VCS 2007', was launched in November of 2007. Projects verified to the pilot version were grandfathered into the 2007 system.

WBCSD/WRI GHG Protocol for Project and Corporate Accounting

The World Business Council for Sustainable Development (WBCSD) and the World Resources Institute (WRI) Protocol for Project Accounting (WBCSD/WRI GHG Protocol) is a widely accepted set of guidelines used by project developers and incorporated into numerous standards, such as the CCAR Protocols and the ISO 14064 standards. The GHG Protocol 'aims at harmonizing GHG accounting and reporting standards internationally to ensure that different trading schemes and other climate-related initiatives adopt consistent approaches to GHG accounting'. This Protocol was created along with a GHG Corporate Accounting and Reporting Standard. Neither the GHG Protocol nor the Corporate Standard is a certification system or verification standard in itself.

Standards for suppliers

Defra's Code of Best Practice for (UK) Consumers and Voluntary Code of Best Practice on Carbon Offsetting

In early 2008, the UK's Department for Environment and Rural Affairs (Defra) launched a Code of Best Practice for Offset Providers based in the UK and 'designed to give consumers clarity and confidence when they choose to offset'. A key feature of this set of guidelines for offset suppliers is the suggestion to customers to only purchase Certified Emission Reductions (CERs), EU Allowances (EUAs) and Emission Reduction Units (ERUs) from 'robust and verifiable' regulated markets rather than VERs from the voluntary markets. However, Defra noted that an endorsement of 'high-quality Voluntary Emission Reductions (VERs) from the non-regulated market' is also under consideration.

Green-e Climate

Green-e Climate was launched in early 2008 and developed primarily to provide certification services for retail providers retiring carbon credits to sell as carbon offsets to customers. This programme requires certification by endorsed project-based standards (including the CDM, the Gold Standard, and the VCS). Green-e Climate certification for carbon offset products aims to ensure that carbon credits are additional as well as independently certified and verified, that project developers and sellers follow accurate accounting practices, and that sellers disclose relevant information about offset sources.

References

Australian Government Department of Climate Change (AGDCC) (2006) *Greenhouse Friendly Consumers* brochure, www.greenhouse.gov.au/greenhousefriendly

Greenhouse Gas Services (2008) 'Greenhouse Gas Services' Standard of Practice', www.ghgs.com/pdf/factsheets/GGSStandards_FS_Final.pdf

Zwick, S. (2006) 'Comparing apples and oranges: In search for a standard for the voluntary carbon market', *The Ecosystem Marketplace*, www.ecosystemmarketplace.com

Websites

CarbonFix Standard: www.carbonfix.info

CCAR Climate Action Reserve: www.climateregistry.org/offsets.html

CCB Standards: www.climate-standards.org

Chicago Climate Exchange: www.chicagoclimatex.com

Defra Code of Best Practice: www.defra.gov.uk/environment/climatechange/uk/carbonoffset/codeofpractice.htm

Gold Standard: www.cdmgoldstandard.org

Green-e Climate: www.green-e.org/getcert_ghg.shtml

Greenhouse Friendly: www.climatechange.gov.au/greenhousefriendly/index.html

ISO 14064/65 standards: www.iso.org

Plan Vivo: www.planvivo.org

Social Carbon: www.ecologica.org.br/ingles/mudancas_social.html

VER+ Standard (TÜV SÜD): www.tuev-sued.de

Voluntary Carbon Standard: www.v-c-s.org

WBCSD/WRI GHG Protocol: www.ghgprotocol.org

World Business Council on Sustainable Development (WBCSD) 'Energy and Climate: GHG Protocol',
www.wbcsd.org/templates/TemplateWBCSD1/layout.asp?type=p&MenuId=Mjc3

Table A2.1 *Examples of standards in the voluntary carbon markets*

Standard	Description	Env. and Social Benefits Req'd?	Registry	Includes LULUCF Methodology?	Geographical Reach	Start Date
Gold Standard for VERs	Certification for offset projects and carbon credits	Yes	APX	Only RE and EE projects	International	1st validated 2006, 1st verified 2007
VCS	Certification for offset projects and carbon credits	No	APX, TZI, Caisse de Depot, own registry	Yes	International	Versions 1 and 2: 2006, VCS 2007:2007
Green-e Climate	Certification programme for offset sellers	No	Registry incorporated	Accepts other standards with LULUCF	International	2008
CCB Standards	Certification programme for offset projects	Yes	Projects on website	Only LULUCF	International	2007
CCX	Internal system for CCX offset projects and CCX carbon credits	No	Registry incorporated w/ trading platform	Yes	International	2003
Plan Vivo	Guidelines for offset projects	Yes	No	Only LULUCF	International	2000
Greenhouse Friendly	Certification programme for offset sellers and carbon neutral products	No	No	Yes	Australia	2001
CAR	A set of protocols and a registry	No	Own registry	Yes	Aimed at US; International soon	CCAR: 2005, CAR: 2008
VER+	Certification programme for offset projects, carbon neutral products	No	TÜV SÜD Blue Registry	Includes a JI or CDM methods	International	2007
ISO 14064	Certification programme for emissions reporting offset projects, carbon credits	No	No	Yes	International	2006
Social Carbon	Certification for offset projects and carbon credits	Yes	TZI	Yes	South America and Portugal	Version 1: 2002 Version 2: 2008
DEFRA	Proposed consumer code for offsetting and accounting	No	No	If CDM/JI approved	UK	2008
Carbon Fix	Design standard for forest carbon sequestration projects	Yes	Projects on website	Yes	International	2007

Offset Registries

This section outlines the major third party registries and registries specific to particular standards, exchanges, verifiers and suppliers as of early 2008. As discussed in Chapter 2, registries are most commonly divided into two functional categories: emissions inventory registries and carbon credit accounting registries. The former tracks buyers' emissions and reductions, whereas the latter reports on transactions of credits, allowances and offsets. This appendix is focused on the latter.

Within the context of carbon credit accounting, the term 'registry' is used both for systems that can serve as the infrastructure for a variety of entities' registry needs and for the distinct registry systems. For example, the California Climate Action Reserve has its own unique registry but APX serves as the infrastructure behind the registry. APX also serves as a project database and one of four registries for the Voluntary Carbon Standard (VCS), as well as for the Gold Standard. Likewise, TZ1 serves both the VCS and the Social Carbon Standard. Alternatively, the TÜV SÜD Blue Registry has its own infrastructure and is the exclusive home for VER+ credits.

Third party registries

APX Environmental Market Depository

APX provides a range of services under the umbrella of 'innovative technology and service solutions' for the energy and environmental markets. For the renewable energy certificate (REC) and carbon markets, the company runs the APX Environmental Market Depository, a web-based platform for tracking, managing and retiring credits. APX currently serves as the infrastructure behind the Climate Action Reserve, the Gold Standard, the America Carbon Registry and the Voluntary Carbon Standards.

American Carbon Registry

The American Carbon Registry, formerly referred to as the Environmental Resources Trust (ERT) GHG Registry, is the longest-standing registry in the voluntary carbon markets. Created in 1997, the registry tracks both 'qualified emissions reductions' and actual carbon credits. Both buyers and suppliers can register tonnes, the credits from which they may either resell or retire. The ERT registry provides third party validation and verification services with standards varying on a case-by-case basis. In March 2007, ERT selected APX to provide technological support for its GHG Registry Program.

GHG CleanProjects Registry

The Canadian GHG CleanProjects Registry's chief objective is to list and de-list GHG reduction projects that result in Verified Emission Reduction-Removal credits (VERRs) for the voluntary and regulated markets. Participants in this Canadian registry may attach a unique serial number to each VERR representing $1tCO_2e$. However, serialization of verified emissions reduction volume is not required. The VERR classification requires adherence to the ISO 14064 standard.

The Registry Company 'Regi'

The Registry Company, known as 'Regi', is operated by M-Co, a private company that works in electricity markets. While the website is tailored to players in New Zealand's voluntary carbon market, it also will consider foreign account requests on a case-by-case basis. Regi accepts VCS and Gold Standard credits. Regi has a high level of transparency, and the general public can visit Regi's website and view the Certificate Summary Listing to find information on offset providers, project names, credit types and volume, and transaction status.

TZ1 Registry

The TZ1 Registry was created to complement the TZ1 Carbon Exchange but is also designed to serve as a third party platform for suppliers and standards registries. For example, TZ1 is one of four registries serving the VCS, serves the Social Carbon Standard and has branched outside of carbon as a registry for the New Forests 'Malua BioBank'. Credits are assigned a serial number, and in addition to tracking trades, the registry will include an externally audited retirement facility for VERs or Kyoto credits. Organizations listing information on the registry are able to choose the level of transparency in their accounts.

Examples of Exchange, Standard and Verifier-Specific Registries

Asia Carbon Registry (ACR)

The Asia Carbon Group (ACG) developed the Asia Carbon Registry for VERs in 2007. ACG provides carbon advisory, finance and asset management services under several different initiatives, namely the ACX-Change and Asia Carbon Asset Development Facility. The Registry plans to accept credits utilizing a variety of standards, including the VCS and the Gold Standard. The scope of registry services includes electronic listing, transferring and eventually retiring VERs.

Australian Climate Exchange Registry

The Australian Climate Exchange (ACX) Registry was developed to track the four types of emissions commodities tradable on the Exchange, namely: Greenhouse Friendly Approved Abatement units, New South Wales GHG Abatement Certificates (NGACs), VER+ credits, and Renewable Energy Certificates (RECs). The Exchange was created initially to serve as a trading platform for Greenhouse Friendly abatement units only, but has since expanded. All credits/certificates listed on the Exchange must first be registered on the ACX Registry, which assesses the credentials of entities verifying the credits according to the methodologies applied, independence from project, and other criteria.

Bank of New York's Global Registry and Custody Service for Voluntary Carbon Units

The Bank of New York's custodial registry was created to become a means of accounting for the Voluntary Carbon Standard's Voluntary Carbon Units (VCUs), and aims to streamline and legitimize the trading process of VCUs. This centralized, electronic and private accounting system stores VCUs, assigns each a unique serial number for tracking and verification purposes, and provides clear parameters for defining account ownership. The registry requires certification under the VCS and account information is not publicly disclosed.

California Climate Action Registry's Climate Action Reserve

The California Climate Action Registry (CCAR) was established by Californian law as a non-profit voluntary registry for GHG emissions aimed at protecting and rewarding companies beyond what regulation requires them to do. Building on its emissions reporting system, CCAR, working with APX Inc, launched the Climate Action Reserve on 14 April 2007 to track and register voluntary projects verified to CCAR protocols. CCAR currently has approved protocols for livestock, methane and forest activities and will soon release a natural gas transmission and distribution reporting and certification protocol.

Chicago Climate Exchange Registry

The Chicago Climate Exchange (CCX) Registry is an accounting system for the CCX's cap-and-trade scheme. Suppliers seeking to include their credits in the registry must first become members and then have their offsets approved by the CCX Committee on Offsets, which then assigns serial numbers to ensuing third party-verified credits. Because both emission reduction allowances and project-based offset credits are traded on the CCX, the registry is both an emissions reductions tracking programme and a carbon credit accounting system. The registry is somewhat transparent, providing publicly available information regarding the offset provider/aggregator, project type and location, as well as transaction volume.

Gold Standard Registry for VERs

In 2008, the Gold Standard Foundation joined forces with APX to create a registry that creates, tracks and enables the transfer of Gold Standard certified VERs, Emission Reduction Units (ERUs) and Certified Emission Reductions (CERs). The registry aims to be a low-cost and transparent electronic database. Information about the status of credits (such as whether they are resaleable or retired) can be accessed by stakeholders who register on the website. The registry features the serialization of each Gold Standard VER credit, a double-entry accounting framework, and full ownership and transaction tracking for VERs, ERUs and CERs.

TÜV SÜD's BlueRegistry

TÜV SÜD, a company that validates and verifies both Kyoto and voluntary emission credits, created the BlueRegistry, a database of certified VERs and renewable energy credits. Currently, the database is exclusive to VER+ credits and RECs. The BlueRegistry is designed to be transparent, and maintains publicly available information on factors such as credit type, credit ownership and vintage.

Retailer registries

Many carbon offset retailers utilize their own registries. Approximately 26 per cent of respondents noted they utilized their own organization's specific registry in 2007 (Hamilton et al, 2008). A select number of these registries are public. For example, The CarbonNeutral Company created its own online registry, which posts detailed information on projects contracted. Dom Stichbury of The CarbonNeutral Company notes that the company does not see its private online registry as a substitute for a third party, multi-company registry. Instead the 'registry was created to be as open as possible about the projects that we've contracted ... and to contribute to increased transparency in the voluntary markets'.

References

Hamilton, K., Sjardin, M., Marcello, T. and Xu, G. (2008) 'Forging a frontier: State of the voluntary carbon markets 2008', The Ecosystem Marketplace and New Carbon Finance, www.ecosystemmarketplace.com

Stichbury, Dom. Interviewed by Katherine Hamilton, July 2008

Websites

APX Environmental Market Directory: www.apx.com

Asia Carbon Registry: www.asiacarbon.com

Australian Climate Exchange Registry: www.climateexchange.com.au

Bank of New York's Global Registry for Voluntary Carbon Units: www.bankofny.com/CpTrust/abo_prs_472.htm

Chicago Climate Exchange (CCX) Registry: www.chicagoclimateexchange.com

Environmental Resources Trust GHG Registry Program: www.ert.net/ghg/index.html

GHG CleanProjects Registry: www.ghgregistries.ca/cleanprojects/index_e.cfm

Globe Carbon Registry: globecarbonregistry.com

Gold Standard Registry for VERs: goldstandard.apx.com

The California Climate Action Registry's Climate Action Reserve: www.climateregistry.org

The Chicago Climate Exchange Registry: www.chicagoclimatex.com

The Registry Company (Regi): www.regi.co.nz

Triodos Climate Clearing House: www.triodos.com/com/climate

TÜV SÜD's BlueRegistry: www.netinform.de/BlueRegistry

TZ1 Registry: www.tz1market.com/registryevolution.php

Table A3.1 *Examples of credit accounting registries in the voluntary carbon markets*

	APX	Bank of New York Registry	American Carbon Registry	TÜV SÜD Blue Registry	CCX Registry	CCAR Climate Action Reserve
Standard/ Verification Requirements	Varies	Voluntary Carbon Standard	ERT approved	VER+ Standard	CCX Board approved	CCAR Protocols
Entities Served	CCAR, VCS, Gold Standard	Voluntary Carbon Standard	Stand-alone system	VER+ Standard	CCX	Stand-alone system
Transparency	Listing requirements public; Some account info public	Standards public; Account info not disclosed	Standards unclear; Majority of account info public	Standards public; Account info public	Standards public; Exchange data public; Account info not public	Standards public; Majority of account info public
Start date	Founded 1996, Registry for carbon credits 2007	2006	1997	2007	2003	Reduction Registry 2003; Certified credit registry 2007

Source: Hamilton et al (2008) *The Ecosystem Marketplace and New Carbon Finance*

Asia Carbon Registry	The Registry Company (Regi)	Australian Climate Exchange Registry	TZI	GHG Clean Projects Registry	Gold Standard Registry
'Approved standards available on the market'	Provisional Gold Standard ISO 14064; greenhouse gas protocol; CDM: JI	ACX approved process, third party accreditation	Varies	ISO14064	Gold Standard
Asia Carbon Exchange	Stand-alone system	Australia Climate Exchange	VCS, Social Carbon, Malua Biobank	Stand-alone system	Gold Standard
Standards public; Unclear if account info public	Standards public; Account info public	Standards unclear; Transaction info disclosed; Account info not public	Listing requirements public; Disclosure of account info varies	Standards public; Account info public	Standards public; Some account info public
2007	2007	2007	2008	2008	2008

Appendix 4

Examples of Offset Suppliers

The following table contains basic information on examples of offset suppliers to the voluntary carbon markets as of late 2008.

Table A4.1 *Examples of voluntary carbon offset suppliers*

Organization Name	Project Type(s)	Location	Website
3Degrees	Livestock Methane, RECs	USA	www.3degreesinc.com
A2G Carbon Partners	Forestry, Renewable Energy	Peru, Spain, USA	www.atwog.com
Action Carbone	Renewable Energy, Energy Efficiency, Waste Methane, Forestry	France	www.actioncarbone.org/ main_fr.php
AGL Energy	Landfill Methane	Australia	www.agl.com.au/Pages/ AGLHome.aspx
AgRefresh [AP-GARM SC, LLC]	Renewable Energy	USA	www.agrefresh.org
Agrinergy Consultancy Pvt Ltd	Mix	Australia	www.agrinergy.com
AIDER	Forestry	Peru	www.aider.com.pe
Ambiental Pv Ltd.	Forestry	Brazil	www.ambientalpv.com
AMCG Ltd (trading as GroPower)	Forestry	USA	www.gropower.net
American Forests	Forestry	USA	
Asja	Landfill Methane, Renewable Energy	USA	www.asja.biz
Atmosclear	Landfill Methane, Forestry, Hydro	USA	www.atmosclear.org
Atmosfair	Renewable Energy, Efficiency	Germany	www.atmosfair.de/index. php?id=9&L=3
Atrium Carbon Fund LP	CCX CFI	USA	www.ricedairy.com/ Sectors/carbon.aspx
Auscarbon International	Forestry, Renewable Energy, Landfill and Waste Methane	Australia	www.auscarbon-intl.com.au

Organization Name	Project Type(s)	Location	Website
Balance Carbon Pty Ltd	Methane, Energy Efficiency	Australia	www.balancecarbon.com
Beartooth Capital Partners	CCX CFI, Agricultural Soil	USA	www.beartoothcap.com
BeGreen (part of Green Mountain Energy Company)	Forestry	USA	www.begreennow.com
BioClimate Research & Development/Plan Vivo	Forestry, Fuel Switching	USA	www.brdt.org
Blue Source, LLC	Mix	USA	www.ghgworks.com
Blue Ventures Carbon Offset	Energy Efficiency	UK	www.bvco.org.uk
Bonneville Environmental Foundation	RECs	USA	www.b-e-f.org
BP targetneutral	Renewable Energy, Methane	UK	www.targetneutral.com
Business for Climate (FACE)	Forestry	Netherlands	www.stichtingface.nl
C-Green Aggregators Inc	CCX CFI	USA	www.c-green.ca
Camco	Renewable Energy, Forestry	Global	www.camcoglobal.com
Canopy (Australian Carbon Biosequestration Initiative Ltd)	A/R	Australia	www.canopy.org.au
CantorCO2e	Mix	USA	www.cantorco2e.com
Carbon Balanced by World Land Trust	Forestry	UK	www.carbonbalanced.org
Carbon Caring	Renewable Energy, Forestry	UK	www.carboncaring.com
Carbon Clear Ltd	Mix	UK	www.carbon-clear.com
Carbon Counter	Renewable Energy, Energy Efficiency, Forestry, Fuel-Switching	USA	www.carboncounter.org
Carbon Footprint Ltd	Forestry	UK	www.carbonfootprint.com
Carbon Impacts	Mix	UK	www.carbonimpacts.co.uk
Carbon Market Solutions Ltd	CCX CFI	New Zealand	www.carbonmarket solutions.com
Carbon Passport Ltd	CERs	UK	www.carbonpassport.com
Carbon Planet	Forestry	Australia	www.carbonplanet.com
Carbon Pool Carbon Conservation	Renewable Energy, Energy Efficiency, Forestry	Australia	www.carbonpool.com
Carbon Reduction Fund	Mix	Canada	www.carbonreduction fund.org
Carbonfund.org	Mix	USA	www.carbonfund.org
Carbonzero	Renewable Energy, Efficiency	Canada	www.carbonzero.co.ca

Organization Name	Project Type(s)	Location	Website
CELB	Forestry	USA	www.celb.org
Clean Air Action Corp	NOx, VOC, and GHG Reductions (via TIST)	USA	www.cleanairaction.com
Clean Air Conservancy	CCX CFI	USA	www.cleanairconservancy.org
Cleaner and Greener (Leonardo Academy)	Mix	USA	www.cleanerandgreener.org
Cleaner Climate	RECs, Mix	Canada	www.cleanerclimate.com
Clear Offset	Biomass	UK	www.clear-offset.com
ClearSky Climate Solutions	Methane, Forestry, Land Use	USA	www.clearskyclimatesolutions.com
Climate Care	Mix	UK	www.climatecare.org
Climate Clean	Mix	USA	climateclean.net
Climate Friendly	Renewable Energy	Australia	climatefriendly.com
Climate Mundi	Methane, Energy Efficiency	France	www.climatemundi.fr
Climate Neutral Group	Waste Methane, Forestry, Renewable Energy, Energy Efficiency	Netherlands	www.klimaatneutraal.nl
Climate Positive	Landfill Methane, Wind	Australia	www.climatepositive.org
Climate Stewards	Renewable Energy, Energy Efficiency, Forestry	UK	www.climatestewards.net
Climate Warehouse	Mix	Brazil	www.climatewarehouse.com
ClimateSAVE	RECs	USA	www.climatesave.com
CO$_2$ Australia Ltd	Forestry	Australia	www.co2australia.com.au
CO$_2$ Neutraal BV	Renewable Energy	Netherlands	www.co2neutraal.net
co2balance.com	Forestry	Global	www.co2balance.com
CO$_2$logic	Renewable Energy, Biomass	Belgium	www.co2logic.com
Conservation International	Forestry	USA	www.conservation.org
Cool Action	Renewables	Canada	www.coolaction.com
CoolClimate LLC trading as AtmosClear	Landfill Methane	USA	www.atmosclear.org
Core Carbon	Fugitive Emissions	Denmark	www.corecarbongroup.com
Correct Carbon Ltd	Forestry, Renewables	UK	www.correctcarbon.co.uk
Credit Suisse	Mix	Switzerland	www.credit-suisse.com
Delta Institute	CCX CFI	USA	www.delta-institute.org
Direct Energy	CCX CFI, Renewables, RECs	USA	www.directenergy.com
DriveGreen	Forestry	USA	www.drivegreen.org

Organization Name	Project Type(s)	Location	Website
Ducks Unlimited	Wetland Conservation	USA	www.ducks.org
DuPont	CCX CFI, Industrial Gas (HFC-23)	USA	www2.dupont.com
e-BlueHorizons	Landfill Methane, Forestry	USA	www.e-bluehorizons.com
E+Co	Renewable Energy	USA	www.eandco.net
EBEX21	Forestry	New Zealand	www.ebex21.co.nz
EcoLogic Development Fund	Forestry	USA	www.ecologic.org
EcoSecurities	Mix	Global	www.ecosecurities.com
EcoVoom	Renewable Energy	UK	www.ecovoom.com
Emergent Ventures India	Renewable Energy, Energy Efficiency, Forestry, Methane	India	www.emergent-ventures.com
Enecore Carbon Limited	Mix	Slovakia, China	enecore.com
EnerGHG India	Renewable Energy, Energy Efficiency, Biomass	India	www.energhg.in
Enpalo	RECs	USA	www.enpalo.com
Environmental Credit Corp	CCX CFI, Landfill and Livestock Methane	USA	www.envcc.com
Environmental Synergy Inc	Forestry	USA	www.environmental-synergy.com/main.html
Envirotrade	Forestry	UK	www.envirotrade.co.uk
Equator LLC	Forestry, Land Use	Americas	www.equatorllc.com
ERA Ecosystem Restoration Associates Inc	Forestry	Canada	www.econeutral.com
Evolution Markets	Mix	USA, Canada, UK, Argentina	new.evomarkets.com
Fieldway International Ltd	A/R	Hong Kong	www.fieldwayinternational.com
Firstclimate (formerly 3C)	Mix	Germany	www.firstclimate.com/en
Flatlander Environmental Services Ltd	CCX CFI, Agricultural Soil	USA	www.flatlander.ca/enviro/home.php
Futuro Forestal	Forestry	Panama, Germany	www.futuroforestal.com
Global Cool	Renewables, Energy Efficiency	UK	www.globalcool.org
Greater Lebanon Refuse Authority	Landfill Methane	USA	www.goglra.org
Green Mountain Energy Company	Renewable Energy	USA	www.greenmountainenergy.com
Greenfleet	Forestry	Australia	www.greenfleet.com.au
Greenland Carbon Trading Private Limited	Renewable Energy, Energy Efficiency	USA	www.greenland-enterprises.com

Organization Name	Project Type(s)	Location	Website
GreenLife	RECs, Landfill and Waste Methane, Natural Gas Pipeline Repair	USA	www.greenlife.com
Greenoxx NGO	CCX CFI, Forestry	Uruguay	www.greenoxx.com/en/ngo.htm
GreenSeat	Renewables, Energy Efficiency, Forestry	Netherlands	www.greenseat.com
GrowAForest	Forestry	UK	www.growaforest.com
Grupo Ecológico Sierra Gorda and Bosque Sustentable	Forestry	Mexico	www.grupoecologico.com
Instituto Ecologica	Mix	Brazil	www.ecologica.org.br/projetos_atuais_hortas.html
LiveCooler	Energy Efficiency	USA	www.livecooler.org
LiveNeutral	CCX CFI	USA	www.liveneutral.org
Meridian Energy	Renewable Energy	New Zealand	www.meridianenergy.co.nz
MGM International	Mix	Global	www.mgminter.com
MoveNeutral	RECs	USA	moveneutral.com
myclimate	Mix	Switzerland	www.myclimate.org
Native Energy	RECs, Methane	USA	www.nativeenergy.com
Natsource	Mix	Global	www.nativeenergy.com
Neco	Mix	Australia	www.neco.com.au
NEOGENPOWER	Renewable Energy	UK	www.neogenpower.com
NetGreen, Inc	Renewable Energy, Livestock Methane	USA	www.achievenetgreen.com
Offset the Rest Limited	Renewable Energy	New Zealand	www.offsettherest.com
Offsetters	CCX CFI, Renewable Energy, Energy Efficiency, Fuel-Switching	Canada	www.offsetters.ca/
OneCarbon	Renewable Energy, Landfill Methane	Netherlands	www.onecarbon.com
orbeo	CCX CFI, ECX	France	www.orbeo.com
Origin Energy	Renewable Energy	Australia	www.originenergy.com.au
Paso Pacifico	Forestry	USA, Nicaragua	www.pasopacifico.org
Pax Natura Foundation	Forestry	USA	www.paxnatura.org
PEAR Carbon Offset Initiative, Ltd	Energy Efficiency, Biogas, Coal Mine Methane	Japan	www.pear-carbon-offset.org/
Planetair	Renewable Energy, Methane, Biomass, Fuel-Switching	Canada	www.planetair.ca

Organization Name	Project Type(s)	Location	Website
PrimaKlima-weltweit-e.V.	Forestry	Germany	www.prima-klima-weltweit.de
PROFAFOR S.A.	Forestry	Ecuador	www.profafor.com
Pure: The Clean Planet Trust	Renewable Energy, Fuel-Switching, Biomass, CCX CFI	UK	www.puretrust.org.uk
Reforest The Tropics	Forestry	USA	www.reforestthetropics.org
Renewable Choice Energy	Renewable Energy	USA	www.renewablechoice.com
Shift2Neutral	Mix	Australia	www.shift2neutral.com
SILVACONSULT AG	Forestry	Switzerland	www.silvaconsult.ch
SKG SANGHA	Renewable Energy, Biogas	India	www.skgsangha.org
Solar Electric Light Fund (SELF)	Off-Grid Renewable Energy	Global	www.self.org
SOS Mata Atlantica	Forestry	Brazil	www.sosmatatlantica.org.br
South Pole Carbon Asset Management	RECs, Energy Efficiency	Switzerland	www.southpolecarbon.com
Southern Metropolitan Regional Council	Renewable Energy	Australia	www.smrc.com.au
Standard Carbon LLC	CCX CFI	USA	www.standardcarbon.com
Sterling Planet	RECs	USA	www.sterlingplanet.com
Sustainable Travel International	Mix	USA, Switzerland	www.sustainabletravelinternational.org
Taiwan Emission Trading Association	CCX CFI, Mix	Taiwan	www.teta.org.tw/EN
Terra Global Capital, LLC	Mix	USA	www.terraglobalcapital.com
TerraPass	Renewable Energy, Methane, CCX CFI	USA	www.terrapass.com
the c-change trust	Forestry	UK	www.thec-changetrust.org
The CarbonNeutral Company	Renewable Energy, Methane	UK	www.carbonneutral.com
The Climate Trust	Renewable Energy, Efficiency, Forestry, Fuel-Switching, Transportation	USA	www.climatetrust.org
The Conservation Fund – Go Zero	Forestry	USA	www.conservationfund.org/gozero
The Global Carbon Reduction Fund	Forestry, Wetlands Restoration	USA	www.carboncontrol.org
The Int'l Small Group & Tree Planting Program (TIST)	Forestry, Agricultural Soil	USA	www.tist.org

Organization Name	Project Type(s)	Location	Website
The Nature Conservancy	Forestry	USA	www.nature.org
The PACE Centre	Renewable Energy, Energy Efficiency	South Africa	www.carbon.org.za
The Trust for Public Land	Forestry	USA	www.tpl.org
The Woodland Trust	Forestry, Agricultural Soil	UK	www.woodland-trust.org.uk
Tradition Financial Services (TFS)	Mix	Global	www.tfsbrokers.com
TreeBanking, Inc	Forestry	USA	www.treebankinginc.com
Treeflights	Forestry	UK	www.treeflights.com
Trees for the Future	Forestry	USA	www.plant-trees.org
Trees for Travel	Forestry	Netherlands	www.treesfortravel.nl
Trees, Water & People	Tree Planting	USA	www.treeswaterpeople.org
Tricorona	Renewable Energy, Energy Efficiency	Sweden	www.tricoronagreen.com
United Nations Development Programme	Mix	Global	www.undp.org
VillageGreen	RECs, Renewable Energy	USA	www.villagegreenenergy.com
Wildlife Conservation Society	Forestry	USA	www.wcs.org
WVO Energy	Renewable Energy	USA	wvoenergy.com
Zerofootprint	Renewable Energy, Forestry	Australia	www.zerofootprint.net
ZeroGHG	Renewable Energy, Landfill Methane, CCX CFI	Canada	www.zeroghg.ca

Note: The offset suppliers listed in this table operate in different levels of the value chain, including project developers, retailers and wholesalers. Many of them also provide advisory services. A/R = afforestation/ reforestation.

Appendix 5

Glossary

additionality
The decrease in CO_2 emissions over and beyond what would have occurred under a business-as-usual scenario. Additionality can be defined in many ways, including financial and regulatory. (See Chapter 2 for more information.)

afforestation
The planting of trees on lands that historically have not contained forests.

allowance
A permit to emit a specified amount of CO_2 or an equivalent greenhouse gas (usually measured in 1 tonne of CO_2e increments) under a cap-and-trade system.

Annex I Parties
Industrialized nation signatories to the Kyoto Protocol. Annex I nations that have ratified their Kyoto agreements are subject to individual emission reduction commitments through 2012. These nations include the 24 original OECD members, the European Union and 14 countries with economies in transition.

Annex II Parties
Nations that have a special obligation under Annex II of the Kyoto Protocol to provide financial resources and facilitate technology transfer to developing countries. Annex II Parties include the 24 original OECD members plus the European Union.

Assigned Allocation Unit (AAU)
A permit to emit 1 metric ton (tonne) of CO_2e under the Kyoto Protocol. AAUs are distributed to Annex 1 countries based on their past emissions. Countries generating fewer total emissions than their allocation of AAUs may sell their excess credits to other Kyoto-compliant nations.

auction
The sale of emission allowances to emitters under a cap-and-trade system.

banking
Storing carbon credits for use in a future year or compliance period.

baseline
The estimate of GHG emissions, population, GDP and other factors that would have occurred without undertaking any climate change mitigation.

biodigester
A waste management tool that captures methane from organic waste as it decomposes and may harness it for later use as a renewable energy source or fertilizer.

brokers
Individuals who facilitate orders to buy or sell carbon credits between suppliers and buyers but do not take ownership of the credits. They typically earn commission based on the size or price of the sale.

cap-and-trade system
An approach used to control pollution by setting a ceiling on total pollutant emissions and providing an economic incentive for achieving emissions reductions. Participants are allowed to trade emissions reduction permits (allowances) in order to make profits from unused allowances or to meet requirements.

carbon credit
A financial instrument equivalent to either (a) the right to emit 1 metric ton of CO_2 or an equivalent GHG (i.e. an allowance) or (b) the reduction or sequestration of 1 metric ton of the same (i.e. an offset).

carbon footprint
A measure of an entity's impact on the environment in terms of the quantity of GHGs emitted.

carbon neutrality
When an individual, firm or government's net carbon dioxide emissions equal zero. This occurs when the amount of CO_2 (or equivalent GHGs) released is effectively neutralized by offsetting the same amount.

carbon offset
A type of carbon credit representing the reduction or sequestration of 1 metric ton (tonne) of CO_2 or an equivalent amount of another GHG. Offsetting involves reducing one's net emissions by buying the rights to emissions reductions generated by projects that reduce GHGs. Offsets are project-based emissions reductions and may be used in the voluntary or regulated markets.

carbon sequestration
The long-term storage of carbon in the biosphere or subsurface terrestrial features in order to reduce its concentration in the atmosphere.

certification
The process of verifying an emission offset to a particular third-party standard and marketing the offset with that particular standard's brand name. For example, carbon offset projects certified by the Gold Standard Foundation can sell their credits through retailers as Gold Standard certified credits.

Certified Emission Reduction (CER)
An emission reduction credit from Kyoto Clean Development Mechanism (CDM) projects (see 'Clean Development Mechanism'), equal to the reduction or sequestration of 1 metric ton of CO_2.

Chicago Climate Exchange (CCX)
A legally binding, cap-and-trade system that members join voluntarily. CCX is the world's first and North America's only voluntary but legally binding, rules-based emissions reduction and trading system.

Clean Development Mechanism (CDM)
One of three 'flexibility mechanisms' of the Kyoto Protocol that allows participating industrialized countries to meet a portion of their reduction obligations by investing in projects that reduce emissions in developing countries. In turn, the industrialized country can earn certified emission reduction (CER) credits that allow it to meet its Kyoto obligations at a lower cost than emissions reductions at home.

double counting
When two entities claim ownership or rights to the benefits of the same emissions reduction.

Emission Reduction Unit (ERU)
An emissions reduction credit from a Kyoto Joint Implementation (JI) project (see 'Joint Implementation'), equal to the reduction or sequestration of 1 metric ton of CO_2 or an equivalent GHG.

emissions trading
A market-based GHG emissions reduction tool that allows entities to buy and sell permits representing the right to emit (allowances) or credits for emissions reductions (offsets). It is one of the three 'flexibility mechanisms' of the Kyoto Protocol.

European Union Allowance Unit (EUA)
The carbon credit traded in the European Union Emissions Trading Scheme (EU ETS). It is designed to be fungible with the Kyoto AAU, allowing entities capped by the EU ETS to offset emissions with credits generated by Kyoto CDM and JI projects.

European Union Emissions Trading Scheme (EU ETS)
The Europe-wide GHG emissions trading system launched in 2005 in response to the Kyoto Protocol. The scheme is the world's first, and largest, multinational emissions trading system.

free allocation
The provision of emission allowances (rights to emit) to entities regulated under a cap-and-trade scheme free of charge.

global warming potential (GWP)
A measure of the atmospheric heat-trapping ability of a given GHG expressed in terms of an equivalent amount of CO_2.

grandfather clause
A legal exception that permits an entity to be exempted from or incorporated into a new legal system.

greenhouse effect
The warming of the Earth's surface and lower atmosphere due to the trapping of infrared energy (solar radiation reflected back into space by the Earth) by atmospheric GHGs. Global warming is believed to be the result of an accelerated greenhouse effect brought on by the increased concentration of atmospheric GHGs.

greenhouse gases (GHGs)
Atmospheric gases that trap heat in the lower atmosphere and contribute to global warming (see 'greenhouse effect'). Some GHGs occur naturally, others are produced only by human activity, and others are produced both naturally and by human activity. The Kyoto Protocol regulates the emissions of six GHGs: carbon dioxide (CO_2), methane (CH_4), nitrous oxide (N_2O), hydrofluorocarbons (HFCs), perfluorocarbons (PFCs) and sulphur hexafluoride (SF_6).

Intergovernmental Panel on Climate Change (IPCC)
An institution whose charter is to evaluate the risk of climate change caused by human activity. It was established in 1988 by the World Meteorological Organization (WMO) and the United Nations Environment Programme (UNEP).

Joint Implementation (JI)
One of the three 'flexibility mechanisms' under the Kyoto Protocol. It allows Annex I Parties to earn carbon offset credits by investing in emissions reduction projects in Annex I countries with developing economies.

Kyoto Protocol
An international agreement on climate change that sets a target for signatory countries' collective emissions reductions and a mechanism for doing so (cap-and-trade). The agreement was reached in 1997 in Kyoto, Japan and came into effect in February 2005. Limits were placed on countries' GHG emissions relative to levels emitted in 1990.

Land Use, Land-Use change, and Forestry (LULUCF)
Under the Kyoto Protocol, a sector of a GHG inventory that encompasses CO_2 sequestration from changes in patterns of land use.

leakage
The 'spillover' of emissions from an entity under some form of a reduction commitment to an entity operating under less stringent regulation. For example, avoiding deforestation in one area could drive deforestation in another area, resulting in no net global carbon benefit.

methodologies
Formal methods, often housed on standards, for addressing various aspects of identifying the baseline, establishing, verifying and monitoring of carbon offset projects. CDM and JI projects must be certified according to the methodologies established by the Kyoto Protocol, whereas offset projects in the voluntary markets may be verified to a number of standardized certification methodologies.

Midwestern Regional Greenhouse Gas Accord
A planned regional regulatory cap-and-trade carbon market encompassing states in the US and Canadian midwest. The accord was signed by nine US states and one Canadian province in 2007.

New South Wales Greenhouse Gas Abatement Scheme (NSW GGAS)
A mandatory cap-and-trade scheme implemented by the regional government of New South Wales, Australia, covering the state's energy industry. Carbon reductions generated by energy producers or third party entities in the form of demand reductions, efficiency gains or sequestration projects are packaged and traded as NGACs (NSW Greenhouse Gas Abatement Credits), each equivalent to a 1 tonne CO_2e reduction.

Oregon Standard
Regulation in the US state of Oregon requiring new large stationary power generation facilities to meet certain standards of efficiency and to purchase off-sets for emissions exceeding these standards. Enacted in 1997, the Standard was the first regulation of CO_2 in the US.

over-the-counter (OTC) market
A set of transactions that are conducted directly between buyers and sellers rather than through a formal trading platform. The voluntary carbon market largely comprises OTC transactions, with companies buying offsets directly from projects or credit brokers.

permanence
The long-term storage of CO_2 in a carbon sink, either through a natural process or through a carbon offset project.

Reduced Emissions for Deforestation and Degradation (REDD)
Emission reductions or foregone emissions achieved through avoided deforestation or avoided land degradation.

reforestation
The planting of deforested areas with new trees.

Regional Greenhouse Gas Initiative (RGGI)
The United States' first regional, mandatory cap-and-trade scheme covering emissions from energy generation in ten northeastern states. The initial auction of emission allowances was conducted in 2008.

registry
An infrastructure for tracking GHG emissions. Registries generally fall into two categories: emission tracking registries (which monitor organizations' emissions and reductions) and carbon accounting registries (which track the verification and sale of carbon credits).

renewable energy
Electricity generated from replenishable sources. This includes traditional wind, solar and hydropower technologies as well as advanced fuels derived from renewable resources, such as algal biofuel.

Renewable Energy Credit (REC)
A tradable environmental commodity representing proof of 1 megawatt-hour of electricity generation from an eligible renewable energy resource.

retailer
A firm that purchases carbon credits from different sources and then sells smaller quantities to voluntary or regulated buyers, often via the internet.

standard
A set of project design, monitoring and reporting criteria to which a given carbon offset project can be certified or verified. Under the Kyoto Protocol, standards for CERs and ERUs are set by the CDM and the JI boards respectively. In the voluntary markets, a number of competing standards have emerged with the intent to increase credibility in the marketplace.

United Nations Framework Convention on Climate Change (UNFCCC)
A framework for intergovernmental efforts in tackling climate change. The Framework was signed at the Earth Summit in Rio de Janeiro in 1992 and it encourages member governments to share information.

validation
The approval of carbon offset projects (either CDM/JI projects under the Kyoto Protocol or projects generating credits for the voluntary markets) at the planning stage. Projects must submit for approval information on baseline scenarios, project design, monitoring scheme, methodology for calculating emission reductions, etc.

verification
The process of verifying emission credits generated by an offset project to a particular standard. In the Kyoto markets, credits from offset projects must be verified through the methodologies outlined under the CDM or JI executive boards. In the voluntary markets, more than one dozen verification standards or project design guidelines exist.

vintage
The year in which an emissions reduction credit is generated.

voluntary carbon market
A market in which firms, individuals and organizations voluntarily buy emission

reduction credits to reduce their net carbon emissions, and which may or may not operate on a formal exchange.

Voluntary Carbon Standard – Agriculture, Forestry, and Other Land Use (VCS AFOLU)

A programme of the Voluntary Carbon Standard to certify carbon credits generated through four categories of land use: afforestation, reforestation and revegetation (ARR); agricultural land management (ALM); improved forest management (IFM); and reducing emissions from deforestation (RED).

Voluntary (or Verified) Emission Reductions (VERs)

General term for offset credits traded in the voluntary markets.

Western Climate Initiative

A planned regional, mandatory cap-and-trade scheme covering (as of late 2008) 11 western US states and Canadian provinces.

wholesaler

An entity that buys emission reductions from smaller offset projects, bundles the credits together and sells them in bulk to institutional buyers.

Index

Printed in the United States
by Baker & Taylor Publisher Services